101
GOLDEN RULES
of
BIRDWATCHING

1 3 5 7 9 10 8 6 4 2

Published in 2009 by Ebury Press, an imprint of Ebury Publishing

A Random House Group Company

Copyright © Quid Publishing 2009

The Random House Group Limited Reg. No. 954009

Addresses for companies within the Random House Group can be found at
www.randomhouse.co.uk

A CIP catalogue record for this book is available from the British Library

The Random House Group Limited supports The Forest Stewardship Council (FSC), the leading
international forest certification organisation. All our titles that are printed on Greenpeace
approved FSC certified paper carry the FSC logo. Our paper procurement policy can be
found at www.rbooks.co.uk/environment

To buy books by your favourite authors and register for offers visit www.rbooks.co.uk

Conceived, designed and produced by
Quid Publishing
Level 4 Sheridan House
114 Western Road
Hove BN3 1DD
England
www.quidpublishing.com

Illustrations: Matt Pagett
Design: Ali Walper

Printed and bound in China
ISBN-13: 978-0-09-193033-2

NOTE
Every effort has been made to ensure that all information contained in this book
is correct and compatible with national standards at the time of publication.
This book is not intended to replace manufacturers' instructions in the use of their products –
always follow their safety guidelines. The author, publisher and copyright holder assume
no responsibility for any injury, loss or damage caused or sustained as a consequence
of the use and application of the contents of this book.

101
GOLDEN RULES
of
BIRDWATCHING

TWITCHING TIPS AND TALES
TO INFORM AND ENTERTAIN

Marcus Schneck

EBURY
PRESS

CONTENTS

📷 INTRODUCTION

Sitting on the icy boulders of a mountain ledge near my home, with freezing winds slicing right through me while waiting for a bald eagle to follow the ancient migratory route that thousands of its predecessors have flown before, the age-old question came to mind: Why bother? No, I really mean it. Sometimes, out there in the field, in miserable conditions, I can find myself questioning the point of life as a birder.

However, even when I'm chilled to the bone, and downcast enough to ponder the question, I can still think of a thousand reasons. Some of those reasons are concrete and easy to quantify; others are harder to pin down, more ephemeral and emotional reactions to birds and birding. But at bottom I know very well why I'm a birder: I love birds.

You'll find many of the reasons why I love birding throughout the following pages. And it has been a thoroughly enjoyable experience for me to retrace all those memories and experiences, and often to remind myself of the many facets

There's so much to see in the world of birding. Even the humble starling, considered a pest by many, can form breathtaking flocks performing stunning aerobatics against the twilight sky.

that make birding such an enjoyable hobby. I hope you enjoy reading them as much as I enjoyed writing them.

How to Read this Book

This is not intended as a field guide, a how-to book, or as some deep discourse on the world's accumulation of birdwatching wisdom. There are, of course, aspects of all these things to be found within these pages. However, taking this book afield with you, while I hope an enjoyable addition to your pack, really won't help you to identify all that many birds. You won't find page after page of projects in this little volume, although I've included a few of my favourites. And, while there is a fair amount of science scattered in these pages, it's only enough to support the rest of the discussion.

If you wish to read this book from cover to cover, then you're more than welcome. But really it's intended as a collection to dip into and out of as you wish. If I had to recommend a place for this book it would most likely be your bedside table, or the breakfast counter, or maybe even the smallest room of your house.

I hope you find something to take away from this book, whatever stage of life as a birdwatcher you may currently occupy. If you're an old-timer, with a life-list as long as your arm – if you don't already know, you'll learn what a life-list is later in these pages – maybe there's something you can still learn, or perhaps a different perspective you might appreciate, or a few thoughts to carry with you in search of your next check-off. If you're a newcomer, there's the perspective of a fair few years in the field, perhaps even with a dash of insight mixed in – not that I, or for that matter any birder, could claim to know it all. And, finally, if you've just picked this book off the shelf in a moment of idle curiosity, and you've never considered birdwatching, then I hope these pages hold just enough inspiration to give you a shove in the right direction.

A Personal Note

I've been pursuing birds for decades and I've written maybe a dozen books about birds, birdwatching and developing habitat for birds. However, I've never written a book quite like this one. Some of the questions posed, and hopefully answered, here never seemed to come up in this exact form in previous projects. For this little tome, the how-to and where-to didn't seem all that important. Instead, I found myself much more often considering the question 'why?'

The life-lists, the rush to see a rare bird, the push to be the first to report a new sighting have never held much appeal for me. It's always been about experiencing the natural world, and that generally includes a good measure of birding.

As a result, I find that I've collected many little tales over the years, a great deal of birding lore, and a bottomless supply of opinion. The pages you're now holding have given me an outlet for sharing of all that ephemera that never found its way into any of my other books. Here I've been able to explore my thoughts, and experience, on subjects as varied as birdwatching luck, the traditions of birding, the pluses and minuses of competitive birding, myths, strange places to find birds and dozens of similarly eclectic topics.

Of course, every birder has his or her own personal collection of tales, tips and tactics. It is my experience, both in the field and as a writer, that has put me in a position fortunate enough to set mine down on paper. But that doesn't mean that they should be considered as definitive. I've put a lot of thought into this project, but I would hate for you to think I'm being overly prescriptive. Almost as much as the huge variety of birds, it is the infinite array of personalities, techniques, history and law that makes birdwatching such a fascinating hobby. Please feel free to disagree and debate my thoughts with your birding friends – after all, these myriad opinions and fierce debates are what moves our pastime forward. I hope you'll pick up a few ideas from these pages, but more than anything I hope it enhances, in some small way, your enjoyment of birds and birdwatching. Good birding!

📷 WHY BIRDWATCHING?

Many of us may not want to admit it, but hunting is hard-wired into our genes. That doesn't mean we all want to rush out, buy the first gun we see and shoot something; it does, however, provide some explanation for the passion that drives many a birdwatcher. If not for the thrill of the chase and finding the prey (albeit for observation, rather than consumption), then what drives so many of us in such an arduous pursuit? For many, birdwatching most certainly is the modern, non-lethal expression of our ancient instincts.

As birdwatchers we may not kill our prey, and in fact we hold a deep concern for its wellbeing; but that is not to say that we are all that different from our primitive forebears. Down through history and prehistory has come evidence that our ancient ancestors held the animals that they hunted in great respect, and even focused elements of their religious lives around these creatures, not least among them birds.

THE WORLD AROUND US
Alongside this respect for wildlife is a shared concern for the environment. It was once the case that humans were a lot closer to the ecosystems in which they lived, and better understood their relationship with them. However, as the centuries have rolled by, advancing technology has both increased the impact of human activity on the planet, and also served to insulate humankind against the consequences.

Now that evidence of the degradation caused to the environment has come to the fore, more and more people are willing to do something about it. At the vanguard of this growing movement are those whose passion for the outdoors means that they have never lost sight of our role within the world around us,

and there are many birdwatchers among their number. People whose day-to-day lives take them beyond the streets of our towns and cities are able to witness human impact on a personal scale and understand what it means for them. From a purely selfish birding point of view, the impact is all too clear: the poorer the environment, the fewer birds we can chase and the fewer enjoyable outings we can look forward to.

On a more positive note, birdwatching also allows us to do something about our concern for the environment. We are able to contribute hard data to an ever wider range of studies, providing scientists with the basis for their research.

THE BENEFITS
We can also find many benefits to our own wellbeing in the pursuit of birds. It takes us out of our air-conditioned homes and offices, and allows us to break away from the stresses of our everyday lives. The rhythms of the natural world help us to relax and also offer a refreshing change of perspective on our own frenetic existence.

If you take it a little more seriously, birding can even provide you with an enjoyable challenge. Waiting for months to catch a glimpse of that elusive bird in your local woods, struggling to make an identification in the driving rain or shooting the perfect photo of a bird in flight can all be a real thrill when you finally get it just right.

Of course, there are also plenty of benefits to our physical health, not the least of which is all that delightful fresh air. The further you take your hobby from your back garden, the greater the potential benefits, and the best birding spots are often at the end of the longest treks. Of course, you don't have to be on foot to get a great workout: why not take a kayak out on the water? The great thing about birding is that whatever your age or ability you can tailor your trips to your requirements.

BIRDWATCHERS OF THE WORLD

The image of the oddly dressed and overly serious lone birder has been a stereotype for a long time – but in reality birdwatchers enjoy company just as much as any other hobbyists. In fact, our hobby is often at the heart of a thriving social scene, with club outings, specialist holidays and now online discussion groups as well.

Birdwatching is also a great way of introducing the next generation to the wonders of nature. Getting kids outdoors and away from the T.V. might seem like a chore at first, but it's often not long before they're hooked, and dragging you out of the door at every opportunity.

So, what kind of birdwatcher am I? Well, I don't maintain lists of all the birds I've ever seen, although I understand why people do. I'm not a great identifier of birds by sight or sound, instead I rely on an array of field guides and recordings to make my field identifications. In short, I am not a world-champion birdwatcher. However, I have been writing about birds and birdwatching for decades, but even now I find that there is still more to learn about them every day.

I make regular treks to see particular species, and, to my family's chagrin, I'm forever pulling off the road to get a better look at a bird, but these decades have taught me that birding is about much more than just ticking species off a list.

So, to return to the original question: why birding? We've already looked at a few good reasons, but there are many more that I hope to unveil throughout the following pages. I hope you enjoy them all.

Far from the eccentric image of old, modern birdwatchers hail from all walks of life, and each pursues the hobby in his or her own way – from the casual backyard birder, to the incurably obsessed twitcher.

THE ART OF PATIENCE

Benjamin Franklin once advised, 'He that can have patience, can have what he will.' The famous dispenser of common-sense philosophy, who proposed that the turkey would be a better symbol for America than the eagle, wasn't known as a great birdwatcher – it's one of the few skills that this renaissance man didn't possess. However, Ben's advice certainly rings true to those of us with some birdwatching experience.

Patience is not only a virtue; it's one of the most important tools in every birdwatcher's toolbox. All things truly do come to he or she who waits... in the right place, at the right time.

Birds, many of them being in the middle of the food chain, are naturally skittish. They are cautious, alert and on their guard against all threats. They are slow to make themselves visible to anything or anyone disturbing their home, or anything they interpret as a threat until circumstances or familiarity indicate otherwise.

The birdwatcher willing to stop and wait will be rewarded, as the quarry slowly returns to its normal routine. A distant call, then another, closer still, will eventually ring out, followed by a glimpse of movement, and then, if you're lucky, a little more.

If waiting a quarter of an hour for some sparrow to show itself seems too great a challenge, then think of those would-be rediscoverers of the ivory-billed woodpecker in the wetlands of the south-eastern United States. These people have spent thousands of hours in search of a species that their detractors insist disappeared into extinction in the 1940s. The hopeful search parties are fuelled by just a few glimpses of birds that may, or may not, be the ones they are seeking.

IN PURSUIT OF PATIENCE

Apart from a short prayer – Lord, grant me patience... now! – patience is skill that must be learned and developed. It can be acquired by simply extending your periods of concentration for longer and longer stretches.

To much of the world, patience is a virtue. To birdwatchers, it is a necessity. Quite simply, great birds come to he or she who waits.

Just sit yourself down on a handy log or bench and force yourself to stay there for quarter of an hour. Move as little as possible and maintain a sharp awareness of everything that is happening around you. Make a clear mental note of everything you notice. Repeat this every day for a week or two, for just a few minutes more each day, until it doesn't feel like a chore.

If building patience proves more difficult for you than can be mastered with that simple exercise, here's a more introspective approach.

First, try to figure out why you are not a patient person. What is it that keeps you from having the patience you require? Take a look inside yourself. Do you have some internal, mental triggers for your impatience? What most often, or most regularly, causes you to lose patience? Look for patterns. Are there some external triggers beyond your control? Look for a way to gain some measure of control over them, at least while you are birdwatching. If all else fails, a few slow, measured, deep breaths can work near-miracles.

And now, because you've been so patient, another quote about patience, this time from the Indian author Eknath Easwaran: 'Patience can't be acquired overnight. It is just like building up a muscle. Every day you need to work on it.' Or, in other words: be patient in your pursuit of patience.

Don't Stress the Birds You're Watching

It's easy to become excited by the probability of seeing a bird you've never seen before; maybe you're even hoping to get a great photograph of it. It's easy to become over eager and then press the bird too closely or too quickly; and then, from the bird's perspective, you have become a source of stress.

As much as we humans dislike stress in our lives, you can multiply that tenfold before you even approach the avian perspective on stress. It's what precedes an attack by a predator of some kind. It's the signal that relocation may be necessary, to leave a favourable spot offering everything you currently need to survive and head off into the unknown in hope of finding something similar elsewhere. It's a drain on hard-to-come-by calories that must now be spent evading the source of stress.

So, the bottom line is to take it easy. Avoid stressing the birds you're watching, and not only will it be better for them, but you will also find the whole experience that much more relaxing and enjoyable yourself.

Today even basic cameras offer lenses powerful enough to keep a good distance from your quarry.

A BRIEF HISTORY OF BIRDWATCHING

As much as 30,000 years ago, an ancient birdwatcher crawled into a cave in what today is Europe and painted a bird on its wall. To be fair, it's not much of a field guide — you can hardly take it anywhere, and it has neither strong field mark references nor species identification keys. However, the image bears lasting testimony to just how long we humans have watched birds and shared our observations with one another.

Those first cave-painting birders and their primitive fellows had the most utilitarian of reasons for watching the birds in their environment. Birds were a source of food and all else needed to sustain life, as well as providing ornamentation for various purposes. Bearing testament to this are the bones of nearly a hundred bird species that have been identified in digs of Stone Age human-occupied sites.

Our fascination with birds may have grown less practical with the ages, but the urge to share our birdwatching observations has never left us.

The ancient Indian Vedas, which were produced from 1500 to 800 BCE, describe nest parasitism by the Asian koel. The Greek philosopher Xenophon, in the third century BCE, mentioned various bird species, including a now-extinct subspecies of ostrich, in his *Anabasis*. Around the same time, in his *Historia Animalium*, Aristotle was publishing notes of bird behaviours such as laying eggs, migration and moulting.

THE FIRST OF THE FIELD GUIDES

In a very early attempt at something akin to a field guide, Pierre Belon, in his *Book of Birds* in 1555, laid down the descriptions of about 200 species. Then, around 50 years later, Ulisse Aldrovandi published 363 volumes on plants and animals, including some 2,000 pages in his *Ornithology*. Later still, in the middle of the seventeenth century, Christopher Merrett set down the first list of British birds, *Pinax Rerum Naturalium Britannicarum*. But how do the writings of that period compare to today's works? Well, to give you an idea, here's a passage from Sir Thomas Browne's 1662 *Notes on the Natural History of Norfolk*.

'A kind of stork was shott in the wing by the sea neare Hasburrowe and brought alive unto mee; it was about a yard high, red head, coulour leggs, and bill, the clawes resembling human nayles, such as Herodotus describeth in the white Ibis of Ægypt.'

This burgeoning interest saw birdwatchers becoming more organised, and the British Ornithologists' Union, one of the oldest such organisations in the world, was founded in 1858.

On the opposite side of the Atlantic, Americans too were putting a great deal of effort into publishing observations. Mark Catesby blazed a trail with the detailed colour plates in his 1731–46 *Natural History of Carolina, Florida and the Bahama Islands*. While a little later, in 1791, William Bartram exploited a European market ready for all things wild and American by publishing a catalogue of flora and fauna of the American South. Then, from 1808 to 1813, Alexander Wilson, the father of American birders, published the seven volumes of his *American Ornithology*. That brings us to John James Audubon in 1820. Hoping to raise his family out of destitution, he coupled his artistic skills with his insight into birds, and set out to document every avian species in America. By 1824, he had drawn enough of the birds to eventually team with London engraver Robert Havell. And, from 1827 to 1838, they produced *The Birds of America*, which included 435 hand-coloured prints. Known as the 'double elephant folio', the tome was produced on vast sheets measuring 29½ in by 39½ in (75 x 100 cm) and featuring life-sized images of the birds – hardly a handy field guide.

THE LAST HUNDRED YEARS

Birdwatching in the early 1900s was in large part dependent upon shooting and collecting specimens for close inspection and careful illustration. It was left to Ludlow Griscom, who led expeditions for Harvard's Museum of Comparative Zoology in the 1920s and

'30s, to give us the concept that birds could be identified without the need to shoot them first.

However, at that time, field guides remained cluttered affairs. That was until Roger Tory Peterson published *A Field Guide to the Birds* in 1934. His pocket-sized guide to birds of the eastern United States used clear and simple paintings of the birds, complete with arrows noting prominent field marks, and unwaveringly accurate descriptions.

More recently, David Allen Sibley, in *The Sibley Guide to Birds*, is credited with bringing about another leap forward. In his new system he arranges multiple images for each species in a way that allows for easy comparisons to be made between the different plumages of one species, as well as between similar plumages of different species.

All this brings us up to date. And while it is clear much has changed, it also evident that, at the heart of our pursuit, much has remained the same.

Cave paintings as old as 30,000 years have been discovered clearly depicting bird-like creatures – stone prototypes of today's birdwatching books perhaps?

👀 EVOLUTION AND DIVERSITY

About 220 million years ago, a group of bipedal dinosaurs known as the theropods (from the Latin for 'beast footed' – think tyrannosaurus and velociraptor) arose to dominate the late Triassic and Cretaceous periods. Their reign continued until about 65 million years ago, when a mass extinction event all but wiped them out, but not before they had given rise to the earliest ancestors of today's 10,000 or so species of birds.

Fossils of archaeopteryx, the oldest known bird – but not, however, a direct ancestor of modern birds – show remarkable similarities to the fossils of theropods including three-toed feet, wishbones, hollow bones, and in some cases feathers and egg brooding. Meanwhile, another example of an early bird in the form of confuciusornis has been discovered more recently in China, although it too is not thought to be a direct link to today's birds. Interestingly, it appears that rather than flying as such, both of these birds may have performed as types of powered gliders.

Archaeopteryx – the oldest known bird.

More recently still, the dromaeosaur cryptovolans has been added to this picture. It was yet another feathered dinosaur, but this time one that appears to have been capable of genuine flight. From this has come the somewhat debated hypothesis that those early feathered dinosaurs archaeopteryx and confuciusornis actually evolved from the first real birds, rather than vice versa; representing the loss of flight in a manner not entirely dissimilar to today's flightless birds.

Regardless of which came first, the bird or the winged theropod, the fossil record seems fairly conclusive that creatures were experimenting with flight at least 150 million years ago.

The debate over the exact origins of today's birds may never be settled; and the fossil record doubtless has many more surprises in store. However, no one debates the remarkably successful diversification and spread of birds across the globe.

When the dinosaurs died out some 65 million years ago – before mammals had evolved beyond a collection of small rodent-like creatures – birds began filling niches around the globe. In certain locations they even appear to have held top-predator status, in the form of the flightless, but aptly named, 'terror-birds' or phorusrhacids.

Evolution and Adaptation

Although the 'terror-birds' failed to hold onto their top spot, that is not to say that other birds have not managed to fulfil niches successfully. The ability to fly and the ever-adapting beak frequently gave new species a competitive edge in their ecosystems.

From the emperor penguins of the Antarctic to the resplendent quetzal of the tropics, birds have evolved to exploit environments of every description. For example, the hummingbirds of the Americas have developed extraordinarily long and narrow beaks, with even longer and thinner tongues, to tap the nectar of flowers. On the other side of the globe, in the New Zealand Alps, the wrybill uses the unique sideways bend of its beak to probe under the edges of boulders. Meanwhile, the widely distributed spoonbill species slash from side to side in shallow waters, creating upward currents that stir up small fish and crustaceans.

The Impact of Us

It's anybody's guess where the next few evolutionary steps will take birds. But, with humans now the predominant species, we most certainly will be a major factor in future developments.

This impact is not all bad, as is the case with the reintroduction of the red kite to England following its previous persecution, and the comeback of the eastern bluebird encouraged by the installation of tens of thousands of nestboxes across the eastern U.S.

However, it is likely that bad news will continue to outweigh good for decades to come. Since 1500 we've lost at least 150 bird species. We're currently losing one bird species per year to habitat destruction, unregulated hunting, the introduction of invasive exotic species, climate change and other factors. Worse still, this rate is projected to accelerate to ten species per year by the end of the century.

The birds with the best chance of making it are those most tolerant of our impact on the planet. Some are even able to prosper in our wake, such as the thriving population of black vultures feasting on the garbage mountains and nesting on the skyscrapers of São Paulo in Brazil, or the reintroduced peregrine falcons hunting for pigeons along the artificial cliffs of American cities.

No one knows for sure what the future holds, but no matter how torrid it may be it is worth remembering that birds survived whatever it was that did for the dinosaurs. Just maybe they can survive us as well.

The installation of tens of thousands of nestboxes across the eastern U.S has seen the bluebird make a comeback.

GETTING LUCKY

Of course, much of birdwatching is to do with luck, being in the right place at the right time. Plenty of people swear by their lucky birdwatching hats, lucky birdwatching boots, lucky binoculars and lucky just about everything else that might be associated with this pursuit that relies so much on the fickle finger of fate.

Talk to any birdwatcher anywhere and time after time they'll refer to the 'bit of luck' that ensured they were looking in just the right place to tick off another species on their life-list, or afforded them a glimpse of the rare species they had driven for hours to see.

Look online and you'll find many a blogger noting the capricious nature in which the gods of birding giveth and the gods of birding taketh away – more frequently the latter, as luck tends to bring the birdwatcher to a prime spot just after a rare bird has moved on.

IT'S ALL IN YOUR MIND

Richard Wiseman, professor of the public understanding of psychology at the University of Hertfordshire, spent years studying luck, both good and bad. In his book, *The Luck Factor*, he demonstrates that all types of luck are the result of human habits that can be measured, defined and often altered.

For example, lucky people tend to be more outgoing and aware, which naturally brings them many more opportunities for good luck to come into play. And, they are also ready to turn whatever comes their way to their own advantage.

Futhermore, these people tend to see the glass as half full rather than half empty, which can help them to find the positive influence of luck where others might see only the bad.

A LUCKY BIRDER

Circumstances like the weather aside, birders really do make their own luck. We can find direction in the advice of Thomas Jefferson, who said, 'I'm a great believer in luck, and I find the harder I work, the more luck I have.'

In the birdwatching world, luck smiles most often and most regularly on those who put in the time and effort to put themselves in the right place at the right time, in the right frame of mind and with the right gear to make the most of the situation.

However, there are times when even the most optimistic among us may find solace in the sentiment of French poet Jean Cocteau: 'Of course I believe in luck. How otherwise to explain the success of some people you detest?'

Finding a four-leafed clover isn't as hard as you might think. Similarly, the luckiest birdwatchers tend also to be the ones who are the most patient and the best informed.

👁 A LESSON IN LATIN

In the fourth century BCE, *before many others had really given it much serious consideration, Aristotle thought a good way to classify animals would be according to how they reproduce and whether or not they had red blood. However, during the boom of zoological discovery in the seventeenth and eighteenth centuries, a system such as that was proven increasingly inadequate, and competing methods did little more than add to the confusion.*

Then, in 1735, Swedish taxonomist Carolus Linnaeus published his *Systema Naturae*, the foundation of the system we still use today. Through various editions and expansions, he built on his original plan until in 1758, in the tenth edition, he classified 4,400 species of animals. Five years earlier he had done the same for 7,700 species of plants.

Every bird has a two-word scientific name in Latin, with the first word indicating genus and the second indicating species, such as Phoenicurus ochruros, the black redstart.

BINOMIAL NOMENCLATURE

The system narrows classification from the broad kingdom – for birds this is Animalia – down to a particular species. It's a system based on binomial nomenclature, in which each species is given a two-part Latin name.

The first part of this two-word scientific name indicates the genus, or group to which the species belongs; while the second identifies the species itself. Thus, the names *Spizella passerina* and *Spizella arborea* reveal that the chipping sparrow and the tree sparrow are closely related, while the song sparrow (*Melospiza melodia*) belongs to a different genus. Using their English names – or, worse yet, their local common names, which can and do vary from one locale to the next – just doesn't offer the same precision.

The binomial system also allows for a subspecies to be denoted by a third word; for example, the eastern chipping sparrow (*Spizella passerina passerina*).

If you're keeping notes, then the convention is to write the scientific name in italics, with the first letter of the genus capitalised. When used alongside the common name, the scientific name is usually written second and placed in parentheses.

When a list of species is presented, all names listed after the first can have the genus abbreviated. For example: *Phoenicurus ochruros, P. phoenicurus* and *P. moussieri* for black redstart, redstart and Moussier's redstart.

🐦 BIRD ANATOMY: A BRIEF INTRODUCTION

Over millions of years of evolution, the anatomy of birds' bodies has incorporated an enormous range of adaptations, a great many of which help birds to get airborne. A lightweight skeleton, including some hollow but strong bones, and light but powerful muscles are two of the key factors that allow birds to fly, and these are aided by circulatory and respiratory systems capable of pumping high volumes of blood and oxygen through the body.

RESPIRATION

Air sacs, which are unique to birds, are central to the high-volume respiratory system. Like bellows, the sacs fill with air and pump it into the lungs, maintaining a steady volume of fresh air throughout the system. When the bird draws in a breath, half of the air directly enters posterior air sacs and half passes through the lungs and into anterior sacs. On exhalation, the air in the anterior sacs is expelled, while the air in the posterior sacs flows into the lungs. With no mixing of oxygen-rich air from the outside and oxygen-depleted air from the inside, it's a very efficient system.

Lacking a diaphragm to power their breathing, birds use their whole body to make it happen, with muscular contraction forcing exhalation.

DIGESTION

The digestive system of many birds has also evolved in a unique direction. Along the oesophagus lies a muscular pouch known as the crop, which stores incoming food and softens it. The crop also regulates the rate at which the food passes through the digestive system, which also includes the gizzard – more technically known as ventriculus. The gizzard is composed of four muscular bands that crush the food and move it along. In some species it's also the place where the bird accumulates small pieces of grit to aid in this grinding process. (It's interesting to note that dinosaurs' digestive systems employed similar mechanisms, leaving behind fossilised gizzard stones known as gastroliths.)

AVIATION

Flight is the most obvious attribute directly enabled by many birds' anatomies. The strong, lightweight skeleton of the bird is central to the equation in the case of birds that can fly. This lightweight structure is based on the fact that many bird bones are hollow, possessing internal structures similar to the trusses in buildings. It's worth noting that large soaring birds like eagles tend to have many more of these hollow bones, while the bones of flightless birds are solid.

Not only must the bones of flying birds be light, they must also be strong, and many are fused. The collarbone – commonly known as the wishbone – is among those; while the heavily developed sternum of the bird also helps support the powerful muscles necessary for flight.

Other instances of extreme fusing in bird bones can be found in the wings, where the carpometacarpus is a fusion of carpal (wrist) and metacarpal (hand) bones, and the hips, where the illium (top of the hip), ischium (side) and pubis (front) are fused into the innominate bone. While the carpometacarpus gives stiff-winged lift and thrust for flight, the

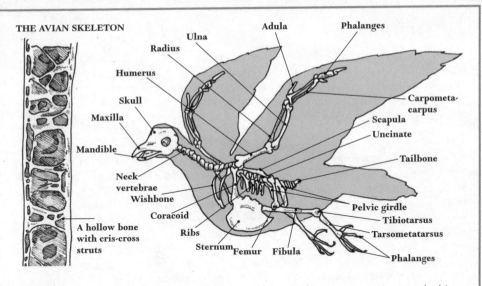

THE AVIAN SKELETON

Adula

Phalanges

Ulna

Radius

Humerus

Skull

Carpometa-carpus

Maxilla

Scapula

Uncinate

Mandible

Tailbone

Neck vertebrae

Wishbone

Coracoid

Pelvic girdle

A hollow bone with cris-cross struts

Ribs

Tibiotarsus

Tarsometatarsus

Sternum

Femur

Fibula

Phalanges

The bird skeleton reveals much about the specialisation of a particular species, not to mention birds' lasting links to the rest of the animal kingdom.

innominate bones allow for egg-laying. Unlike the fused bones elsewhere, birds have more neck vertebrae – from 13 to 25 – than many other animals, giving them incredibly flexible necks.

Around their unique skeletal structures, most birds have about 175 muscles. The largest of these, at least in those birds capable of flight, are the pectorals (breast muscles), which power the dynamic downstroke of the wings. So crucial are these, that they account for some 15 to 25 percent of the bird's weight. Providing the upward pull on the wing is the ventral or supracoracoideus muscle, weighing another 10 percent of the bird's total mass.

THE BEAK

In harmony with the lightweight bone structure is the absence of a jawbone.

Without teeth to support, birds have evolved beaks, which are much lighter than the jawbone–teeth arrangements in other animals. Although a defining feature of birds, it is, however, worth noting that other creatures – for example, the squid – possess similar mouthparts.

The beak has a hard sheath of keratin called the rhamphotheca, while inside is porous bone with a layer of blood vessels and nerves between. Also, a pair of holes called nares, lead from the outside to the respiratory system, where we began.

That completes our whistlestop tour of a bird's anatomy. There are many generalisations and omissions necessitated by the brevity of this entry, but I hope to have piqued your interest. After all, it can only enhance your viewing to know what lies beneath your quarry's beautiful plumage.

🔭 MIGRATION

Migration is the billboard of birdwatching. Nothing has done more to attract new converts to the hobby than the passing flocks at the change of seasons. For birdwatchers and non-birdwatchers alike it's hard to remain unmoved by one of nature's great spectacles, especially when species that are unheard of through much of the year suddenly start showing up in our gardens.

Small migrations are often made as a response to changes in food supply, habitat or short-term weather. However, we usually employ other terms for those movements, such as 'irruption'. The term migration is more commonly reserved for the big seasonal movements, most often south in the autumn to warmer regions and north in the spring to temperate or Arctic regions. The southern terminus is known as the wintering ground, while the northern terminus of the migration is the breeding ground.

While this might well sound straightforward, many questions are raised by species in which not all members are migratory. Partial migration, as it is known, is not uncommon. For example, kestrels on both sides of the Atlantic exhibit behaviour in which some parts of the population are migratory, some are migratory over only short distances, and others are resident. Some of the migrating kestrels may even leapfrog over resident groups. To complicate the picture further some species exhibit gender-specific migration, as is the case with the chaffinch in Scandinavia; only the females migrate, with the males remaining in their territories.

PROS AND CONS OF MIGRATION

From the point of view of those birds that undertake it, seasonal migration is a risky affair, and each bird expends a lot of energy making the trip. It's also putting itself under a lot of stress as it ventures through new, often inhospitable places filled with would-be predators waiting to feed on the passing buffet.

Nevertheless, migration is also the route to the most bountiful supplies of food. In the north, the longer days of spring through summer are packed with opportunities for birds to feed their demanding hatchlings and build their own reserves. Migratory species are better able to raise large clutches than they would in the tropical regions, where the food supply varies little over the year. Then, when the northern pantry begins

Record Holders

The Arctic tern is the long-distance migration record-holder, managing one-way movements of 14,000 miles (22,500 km). The sooty shearwater travels about 9,000 miles (14,500 km) between breeding grounds in the Falkland Islands and Norway, while the Manx shearwater makes pretty much the same trip in the seasonally opposite direction.

Passing flocks of migrating birds are among the clearest signals of changing seasons for everyone living in the temperate regions of the world.

to dwindle in late summer, the migrants move south for what is now an easier life.

Migration generally follows historic routes, such as along coastlines, major rivers or mountain ranges. These routes are known as 'flyways', and they generally provide the migrants with a helping hand, whether in the form of updrafts, beneficial wind patterns or seasonally abundant food supplies. And, because the benefits of a given route will change with the seasons, the birds often use different ones on their trips north and south.

BIRDS OF A FEATHER

Flocks are the most familiar travelling arrangement. The V formation of geese, for example, is known to even those who are not at all interested in birdwatching. For the birds, they provide an aerodynamic advantage, requiring less energy of each individual than it would expend making the journey on its own. There is growing evidence that group flight also allows for a faster trip. However, there are always exceptions; not all birds migrate in flocks, and some filter along the route individually.

As well as the routes, the altitudes at which birds fly also vary considerably.

Bar-headed geese have been documented flying over the tallest peaks of the Himalayas, at about 29,000 ft (nearly 9,000 m); while, at the other extreme, migrating seabirds skim the waves. Most migration, however, takes places between 500 and 2,000 ft (150 and 600 m).

THE TRIGGERS OF MIGRATION

Migration is triggered by environmental changes – most notably the changing length of day. However, it is worth noting that not all migration takes place during daylight hours. For example, a spectrographic study in the U.S. documented 35 different night-flying species of migrant.

A species' response to these triggers relies in part upon its genetic conditioning, but this does not provide a full picture. One famous example being a flock of whooping cranes that was trained to follow a migration route behind a microlight.

Even then our knowledge of the processes taking place in birds' brains and the way they relate to the Earth's magnetic fields is greatly lacking. We are left with little choice but to gaze in wonderment.

👓 LOOKING FOR FIELD MARKS

Field guides, birding writers, bird-trek leaders and others will all tell you, time and again, to check out the field marks to make your bird identifications. Of course, that's only possible if you understand them in the first place. So here's a brief introduction to using field marks.

To start with you need to know the topographical regions of the bird: beak, head, back, wings, tail and legs.

THE HEAD
Important field marks of the head are the eyebrow stripe, which runs above the eye; the eyeline, which runs through the eye; the eyering, which encircles the eye; the crown stripe along the centre of the head; the lore area between the beak and the eye; the whisker mark, where the bird's whiskers would be if it was a cat; overall beak; the upper beak; the lower beak; and the throat patch.

THE WINGS
Field marks are somewhat simpler on the wings, although equally important. Even when the bird is in non-breeding

The use of field marks in identifying birds may appear very complicated to newcomers, but it soon becomes second nature.

plumage, the field marks on the wing will help with identification. Primary wing field marks include wing bars and wing patches.

TAKING IT ALL IN
Many professionals recommend that field-mark identification begins with the head, moving down over the back to the wings, rump and tail. Then back to the head, considering the beak and the throat before moving to the breast, belly, legs and underside of the tail.

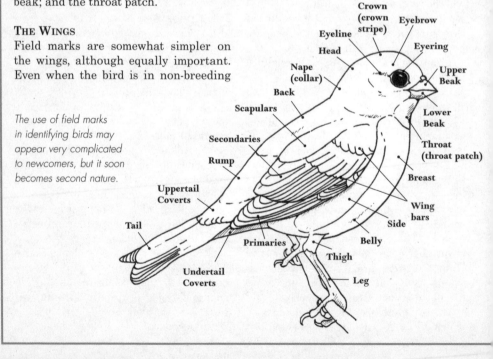

Crown (crown stripe)
Eyebrow
Eyeline
Head
Eyering
Nape (collar)
Upper Beak
Back
Lower Beak
Scapulars
Throat (throat patch)
Secondaries
Rump
Breast
Uppertail Coverts
Wing bars
Tail
Side
Primaries
Belly
Undertail Coverts
Thigh
Leg

PETERSON AND BEYOND

Although the concept of field marks was known for years before, Roger Tory Peterson, in 1934, elevated them to the level they hold with birders today. In his *Field Guide to the Birds*, Peterson introduced his 'Peterson System', which simplified the artwork images of the birds to emphasise the field marks, used arrows to pinpoint the critical marks and grouped birds of similar appearance together to facilitate differentiation. Peterson moved in the same direction with his narrative, eliminating long passages of description to make way for shorter, more direct lines concentrating on the important field marks.

While Peterson developed the system, he got the idea from Ernest Thompson Seton's book, *Two Little Savages*, in which one of the principal characters tried to capture the field marks of distant ducks to aid in his identification of them. Seton included sketches in his book not unlike those later produced by Peterson.

Many believe David Allen Sibley took the Peterson System to its next logical level in 2000. He used the pointer system for key field marks, but added annotations to further facilitate accurate identification, and then beefed up the text in each entry to provide more detailed description. Sibley also includes more illustrations that show plumage variations by age, sex and geography for any given species. And, his range maps, while being highly detailed, also include indications of spots where the birds are rare but regular.

📻 BIRDWATCHING FOR CHARITY

As we'll note later, the competitive events of birdwatching often take place in the name of charity. And, smaller, less formal events have also been developed, often to coincide with the big ones.

Such charity competitions often take the form of being sponsored for every species you watch. However, there are a number of other ways to combine a passion for birding with raising money for charity.

I guess the most obvious of these is the fees that we pay to follow our passion, whether in terms of annual subscriptions to birding organisations, or the admission fees that we pay on entry to a bird conservancy.

Furthermore, many field guides are affiliated with a charitable birding organisation – with a percentage of the profit from sales going to that organization. In a similar vein, many charities publish their own Christmas cards or postcards, and you will often find they have shops either online or at their conservation centres – most often both.

Beyond this are the special events that are organised on behalf of charities, such as auctions and the like. And, finally, there's your own hard-earned cash. You'd pay to watch a movie, or go to the theatre, so why not set a little aside each time you venture out in search of birds and make a donation to those organisations who are fighting to ensure they'll still be there in years to come.

🔭 COURTSHIP

Some birds, such as male robins and mockingbirds, are incredibly aggressive in their defence of breeding territories, often battling it out until one of the combatants is injured. Their wing-beating, body-slamming attacks on rivals are awesome to witness, and speak volumes about the deeply ingrained desire to pass on their genes.

The world of birds is filled with species that begin their courtship period with an active defence of their territory; the better their territory, the better their breeding opportunities. However, that is not the whole picture, and there are also many species that engage in very little pre-courting warfare. One example of this is the mute swan, which generally retains the same partner so long as the two of them live. It's easy to romanticise the relationship, but in reality the demise of one of the pair will see the surviving swan taking up with a replacement mate.

SURVIVAL OF THE FITTEST
It might look shocking, but the battle for courtship and mating rights is no bad thing. It's nature's way of ensuring, in general, that only the fittest of the species will pass on their genes and thus continue the line with strong, healthy offspring that in time will do the same.

Exactly the same genetic imperative has led to myriad courtship displays and rituals. In a great many species, the female chooses her mate based partly on the appearance and actions of the male. In practice this can mean choosing the male with the brightest, most colourful feathers; the male with the most complex gyrations and movements; the male with the best territory; the male with the most well-built or elaborate nest or courtship grounds; the male that offers her the tastiest morsels; the male able to subdue her; or in many cases a combination of these factors. (If you think about it, it's pretty clear that we humans still find many similar attributes attractive and that we still haven't shaken entirely free of our own genetic imperatives when it comes to courtship.)

It is this evolutionary one-upmanship that provides many of birdwatching's most enduring sights: the elaborate tail of the male peacock; the decorated mating field of the bowerbird; the energetic zigzag courtship flights of the American woodcock.

However, in spite of all these efforts there are those species in which the female will mate with several males, just as there are those in which the male is the hit-and-run artist. For the birds it's all about passing their genes on to the next generation, and, to be frank, anything goes.

🔭 BIRDWATCHING IN THE FUTURE

Despite its occasionally staid image, birdwatching has benefitted just as much as any other hobby from the technological revolution of the computer age. In this regard at least the future of birdwatching is bright, but let's gaze into our crystal ball to see what the world of tomorrow will hold.

Perhaps binoculars, the basic tool of the birdwatcher, will become self-contained digital information systems. Their magnification abilities will be incredible, they will also register audio inputs and help set the song of a bird apart from the background noise. They will link wirelessly to tiny GPS-equipped computers, which will carry huge amounts of personal data into the field and send that information around the globe. They'll also probably be much lighter and more compact than today's models, and maybe even have solar-cell technology to power them.

Environmentally, however, things are not looking as bright. There will be fewer species of birds in more isolated and more degraded environments. We'll be posed energy and lifestyle questions to which the answers will not come easily. Pressures to serve human needs to the detriment of all other life on the planet will continue to grow. While conservation organisations will be swamped by the sheer breadth of need, and be forced to focus narrowly on that which can still be saved.

COSTS AND BENEFITS

As technologically advanced as we will become in the future, many people will be wrapped up in the electronic culture that is already engulfing us. And making the problems facing the environment seem real is going to be increasingly difficult. Unfortunately, this is at the same time a near-revolution is needed to have any chance of limiting the devastating impact that we have had around the globe.

In a world where many environments are in decline, the future may well hold far fewer birds for us to watch, meaning many more of us will be eager to share in each and every sighting.

🔭 NESTING INSTINCTS

From a bird's perspective, a nest is a safe place to lay its eggs and raise its young. Different species have evolved to employ widely differing methods and designs to meet those same basic requirements, and individuals are genetically programmed to follow the examples employed by their parents. For most birds the building of the nest will be some of the hardest, most exacting work they will ever do.

A few species go to great lengths in the preparation of their nests. Male weaver birds derive their name from the elaborate baskets of long grass stems that they weave, while male bowerbirds are constantly working to improve and decorate their bower of sticks and stems. Meanwhile, in Southeast Asia, tailorbirds use their long, sharp beaks like needles to sew together leaves with plant fibres and make funnel-shaped nests. All have strong incentives, as the females of the species make their mating choices based on how well they fancy the end results.

Spectacular as these nests are, perhaps the strangest arrangement is employed by the hornbills. The female builds her nest in a tree cavity, and then her mate seals her in, leaving just a small hole through which he passes her and her hatchlings food. It's the most protected nest there is, albeit somewhat claustrophobic from a human perspective.

WHAT'S IN A NEST?

The most common type of nest is the simple cup or bowl. It might be cemented together with mud, and is often lined with fine grass or some other soft material.

Some species incorporate specific materials; for example, hummingbirds and woodstars build perfectly shaped, thimble-sized cup nests attached to the tops of branches using moss and cobwebs. While the female song thrush likes to mix her nest-building mud with dung and rotten wood.

Perhaps the strangest of the cup-type nests are those of the edible-nest swiftlet, which consist almost entirely of hardened saliva. In fact it is these nests that are most often used in the infamous 'bird's nest soup'. Although the nests are gathered through a labour-

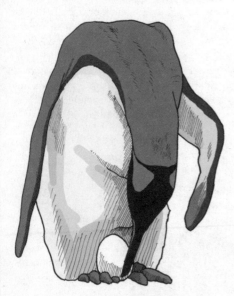

Nesting behaviour varies widely among species, from the penguins who carry their eggs on their feet to hornbills that seal the female in with the eggs until they hatch.

intensive process in which collectors perch precariously on ladders set up along the sides of cliffs, thousands are still taken every year. Some naturalists believe the birds may be extinct in less than a decade.

LIFE WITHOUT A NEST

Alongside the almost infinite variety of nests are many species that simply don't make one. Perhaps the most famous example is that of penguins, who carry their eggs on their feet, pressed into the warmth of their belly feathers. Another is the killdeer, which just clears a spot in some gravel, lays her eggs and then relies on the natural camouflage of those eggs and the broken-wing decoy tactics of the parents to keep predators at bay until the hatchlings emerge.

There are also those species, like bluebirds and owls, that take things as they find them, looking for a hole in a fence post, tree or nestbox. While woodpeckers also like to nest in holes in trees, but are equipped with the tools to make their own and produce the sawdust and wood chips to line them.

More sinister, at least to our human sensibilities, are those birds that freeload on others' hard work. Sparrows will take over nests built by other birds, such as martins, push out the parents' eggs, lay their own and set up house. While some, like the black-headed grosbeak, will actually steal pieces of other birds' nests to use in their own constructions. Meanwhile, nest parasites, such as the cuckoo and cowbird, lay their eggs among those of other birds and leave the hard work of hatching and raising their offspring to someone else.

The Biggest Nests

The sociable weaver bird of the Kalahari Desert in Africa is the king of the giant nest. However, it is only by building colonies of nests that they can sometimes come up with structures weighing more than a metric ton. If, however, you're looking for the work of a single pair, then look no further than the bald eagle. One of the largest eagle nests ever documented was 9½ ft (2.9 m) in diameter and 20 ft (6.1 m) deep, and weighed nearly three tons. Tree branches the likes of which you and I would consider fine campfire wood are prime nesting materials for the eagle. The reason why: A pair of bald eagles will use the same nest year after year, adding to the construction every time, so it makes sense to build something substantial.

FEEDING

To understand evolution, look at bird beaks, after all that's what Darwin famously did with the finches of the Galapagos. Like a well-equipped handyman's workbench, the world of birds is filled with specialised tools, each one designed for a specific task; adaptive evolution has supplied birds with a wide array of food-gathering tools to fit the various niches of any number of ecosystems.

IF THE BEAK FITS

The size and shape of a bird's beak is indicative of the food it eats:

+ Short, thick, conical beaks, like those of finches and sparrows, are designed for cracking open seeds and extracting the kernels inside the hulls.
+ Thin, slender, pointed beaks, such as those of warblers and wrens, are used to pluck insects from twigs, bark and leaves and from among plant litter on the ground.
+ Long, heavy, chisel-like beaks – the tool of woodpeckers – are built for drilling holes into trees to get at insects that live under the bark.
+ Long, delicate, tubular beaks, such as those of hummingbirds, are often associated with even longer tongues and a penchant for sipping nectar from flowers.
+ Large, heavy, slightly curved, but conical beaks, like those of crows, provide their owners with the ability to take advantage of a wide range of foods.
+ Long, flat, fringed beaks – the equipment of many ducks and other waterfowl – are designed for straining food from water.
+ Sharp, hooked beaks, like those threatening tools carried by hawks and owls, are used to catch, kill and rip apart live prey.
+ Long, pointed, spear-like beaks, carried by herons and kingfishers, are also adapted to live prey, but this time for spearing and gulping it down.

BACKYARD BIRD FEED

Armed with the above information you should be able to make well-informed choices among different types of seeds and mixes available. However, it's also worth noting some of the studies that have been made since bird feeding became a huge industry in the last quarter of the twentieth century.

Chief among those researchers has been Aelred Geis of the U.S. Fish and Wildlife Service. He has determined, and many others have confirmed, that black oil sunflower is the preferred seed for the largest variety of backyard birds, nearly all of them as a matter of fact. White proso millet pretty much fills in the gaps for the rest of them. In addition, niger seed is a preference among some finch species. In the States cardinals really like safflower seed, especially when offered in a bin-type feeder near the escape cover of evergreens. While peanuts in the shell are a favourite with jays and crows.

Now, read the contents label on your usual seed mix, and while you do so, it's worth noting that researchers have determined that wheat, milo, peanut hearts, oats and rice are on almost no species' most-wanted menu.

Although the basic bird feeder types are fairly well set, new variations are developed and marketed every year by the myriad birdwatching supply companies in pursuit of your hard-earned cash.

SERVING SEED

Regardless of your preference in seeds for feeding your garden birds, it's essential to keep the seeds fresh, dry and free of mould. Birds will reject spoiled seed or old seed. How the seed is offered is also critical. Most species will be well served by hanging tubes and bin feeders, with the smaller species showing a real preference for the tubes.

And, of the remaining species, nearly all will take seed from the ground or an elevated platform.

SUET

Suet is a special addition to the backyard buffet. At one time it was specifically raw beef fat, while tallow was the term for beef fat that had been rendered, which involves melting the fat and allowing it to re-solidify into a form that will store better. Today, in bird-feeding circles at least, suet is generally taken to mean either form – regardless of the terminology, it is high in calories and high in protein. It is most often offered in commercially prepared cakes in wire cages, although an increasingly popular practice is to dip pine cones into melted suet, let them dry and then hang them out for the birds (see p. 70).

Many guides warn that suet should not be made available at temperatures approaching 70° F (21° C) because it will turn rancid. However, the process of double rendering will bypass that concern. It's quite simple to double render suet; just melt it once, allow it to solidify and melt it again. Then it's ready for use in any weather.

Suet can also be used in the raw form, in strips cut right from the cow. Many meat counters and butchers have recognised the additional profit they stand to make by offering something that was once considered a waste by-product to the birding market.

Because feeding garden birds is among the most direct interactions any birdwatcher will experience, it's an activity that is ripe for experimentation. This gives you the chance to tinker endlessly, inviting a great variety of species to feast at your buffet.

🔭 SELECTING FIELD GUIDES

If you're new to the passion of birdwatching, you may not view your field guides as anything much more than books. However, like your binoculars, your field guides are serious tools. A bad choice of guide will most likely leave you scratching your head as the most interesting sights of the day pass you by.

Publishers have not made the choice of guide any easier, as they have churned out an incredible variety of books. There are dozens of poor guides out there, but a far more limited selection of really first-rate ones.

What Makes a Good Guide?

I'll resist the temptation to prescribe a single 'best guide' because that one-size-fits-all approach just doesn't work. The bottom line is that a good field guide is one that suits your personal preferences, and you'll only find out what these are through personal experience. However, in case you are thinking about buying your first field guide, or don't have years of experience to draw on, here are a few pointers to help you along the way.

The guide should cover the geographic area where you want to do your birding. Don't be tempted to use a guide you already have, but is intended for a nearby area, as it will often be of extremely limited value. Regionalised guides are currently in vogue with publishers, and you should be able to find a well-executed guide designed for your area that will offer more useful information that a nationwide book ever could.

Similarly, the guide should cover all the birds in the area. Guides designed to cover just one group of birds usually offer much greater detail, but leave huge gaps that become painfully obvious when you come across a bird not in that group.

That said, group-limited guides are useful, and are well worth considering when your birdwatching efforts become more advanced and more focused.

Often overlooked is the 'field' part of the guide. It should be small enough to be easily portable, but large enough to carry detailed information. Waterproof or weatherproof construction is a bonus, but doesn't justify buying a bad guide just because it will last a long time.

Whether you should choose a guide with photos or illustrations is again down to personal preference, but well-done artwork is generally more helpful when making identifications. While artwork can highlight important field marks, photos are based on just one individual, which may or may not be completely representative of its species and almost certainly will not be representative of the opposite sex. One caveat, though, is that poorly done artwork, of course, can be worse than useless.

Buying the Guide

Bookstores are the best places to shop, because you will be able to pick up and compare all the different guides and their various aspects. Most stores will have a selection, although probably not the range that is available through the big online outlets. Prices will also be a little higher, but if that is really a deal breaker for you then you can always look in-store and buy later online.

📷 SHARING BIRDS WITH OTHER BIRDERS

In the growing shadow of the internet, anything can be shared in the blink of an eye. The precise GPS coordinates for the location of an incredibly rare bird can be beamed around the globe within moments of the first sighting. Others can then make their way to the spot, using very little in the way of traditional birdwatching skills along the way. In some cases they don't even need to leave their computers, as remote cameras can record a bird's every movement. All this changing technology poses tough questions when it comes to whether or not you should share your sightings.

A scene from the blockbuster *Jurassic Park* comes to mind. Mathematician Ian Malcolm (played by Jeff Goldblum) and park owner John Hammond, (Richard Attenborough) are debating the merits of bringing dinosaurs back into existence. Hammond argues, 'You don't give us our due credit. Our scientists have done things no one could ever do before.' To which Malcolm responds, 'Your scientists were so preoccupied with whether or not they could, they didn't stop to think if they should.'

CAN WE OR SHOULD WE?

It's a line I find myself quoting in many discussions about the current march of technology. And, again, it applies here. Passing information along from birdwatcher to birdwatcher has been a hallmark of our passion for a couple of centuries. It was also one of the primary motivations of the earliest writers on the subject.

In the past there was never any question about the tradition of sharing birds with other birdwatchers. But now technology has changed the rules of the game. We can communicate at such speed across huge distances and to so many people at the same time that the question of whether we can share information about our sightings has been replaced by the question of whether we should.

News of the sighting of a rare bird spreads rapidly, sometimes attracting extremely large crowds of birdwatchers, to the detriment of the bird and the environment.

🔭 BIRD PHOTOGRAPHY

The digital age has brought a new number-one rule to bird photography: Shoot a lot of frames of everything and then shoot some more. The elimination of film and photo processing has made it a no-brainer. If in doubt, take a shot, then you can sort the wheat from the chaff later on computer. That doesn't, however, excuse poor technique – putting just a little thought into your shots will pay great dividends.

Although additional levels of quality can still be attained by investing in more advanced equipment with interchangeable lenses and the like, today's digital point-and-shoot cameras can take a photo that's good enough for most of us.

Many also pack relatively powerful lenses, given their size, and combined with the level of automation they offer, even the greatest of technophobes would be hard-pushed to find a reason not to slip one into their pocket.

Of course, if you want to exert greater creative influence then you should look at investing in a camera that offers you

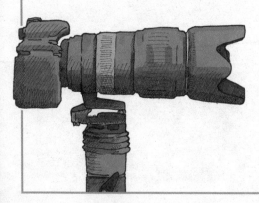

For an aspiring bird photographer, an SLR with its interchangeable lenses and vast array of variable controls is the ideal camera. For most of us, however, a digital compact that slips into the pocket is more practical.

greater control over exposure and focus, as well as a range of other variables.

More advanced cameras offer plenty of special controls and settings in addition to the basics of aperture and shutter speed, but all that information is best left to a book about camera technique. Instead, let's concentrate on the skills that can be applied regardless of the kit you're packing.

COMPOSITION

In general, in any photo showing a single bird – or for that matter in any kind of portrait, animal or human – the main point of focus should be the eyes. If the eyes are a little blurred then this will almost certainly detract from your image's impact.

In order to make sure the eyes are nice and sharp you can use the focus lock that most cameras offer. This usually involves pointing the camera at the subject then semi-depressing the shutter-release button to focus, then keeping the button semi-depressed and recomposing the frame as you wish.

Furthermore, if you're having trouble keeping a steady hand, or you're using a long lens, then steady your camera on a tripod, or a less bulky monopod. Alternatively, a beanbag on a car roof or a low wall will also do the trick.

If the bird is on the move, whether on the ground or in the air, then another

Think about how you use colour in your photographs. You don't always have to shoot in full colour, and you can even change your photos on computer. Why not try some black-and-white shots, or perhaps the old-fashioned browns or blues of a sepia or cyanotype setting?

good rule is to leave plenty of space in front of it in the frame. Not only will this prevent you clipping its beak and spoiling the shot, but it will also help create a more natural feeling to the image, in which the bird doesn't appear cramped by the frame's edge.

In addition, there's also the tried and tested 'rule of thirds'. Looking through the viewfinder, imagine two equally spaced horizontal lines and two equally spaced vertical lines running through the rectangular image. Then place important features along these lines, or at the points where they intersect. As always, rules exist to be broken, but this simple trick improves many shots.

COLOUR AND LIGHT

Whenever possible, try shooting at either end of the day. This often lends a nice warm glow to the light, which simply isn't there in the middle of the day. It is also better for retaining some detail in shadow areas, as, for that matter, is the light on a cloudy day. If you must shoot during the height of day, consider using flash – you might not need it to illuminate the whole subject, but it can even out the shadows somewhat.

Finally, think about colour. Digital capture gives you a great opportunity to play around with saturation and brightness, or even switch the whole shot to monochrome at the click of a mouse.

🔭 THWARTING CATS

It's all about food. We offer food to attract birds to within viewing range in our gardens. However, in doing so we unintentionally offer the birds as an attraction for local cats.

Often a congregation of birds will also attract hawks and other natural predators, but there are real differences between those natural predators and free-roaming house cats. Many of us in the birding community share the perspective that house cats are not a natural part of our ecosystems and we are therefore pretty intolerant of their predation.

Trying our patience even further is many cats' penchant for killing even when they are well-fed and in no need of a meal. We all know of house cats that regularly deliver dead birds to the feet of their owners. Indeed, many of us have such a cat and are torn by the conflict between a dearly loved pet and much-valued wildlife.

THE FACTS OF THE MATTER

Cats cause more bird deaths than any other animal, wild or domestic; and various studies have demonstrated that an individual allowed to roam outdoors can kill as many as a thousand wild animals each year. On the other hand, many cats never develop the necessary hunting skills to catch birds.

Furthermore, the debate about the impact of this predation still rages. For example, in the UK, the Royal Society for the Protection of Birds (RSPB) admits that there is no scientific evidence that the large number of birds killed by cats actually affects the population at all – as the birds caught tend to be weak or sick and would have died anyway. On the other hand, a study in the San Diego area in the U.S. unveiled evidence for the role of free-roaming cats in the local extinctions of several native bird species, including the cactus wren, California quail and roadrunner.

A balanced perspective seems to be that populations of those garden species most likely to be preyed upon tend not to suffer unduly. However, when cats are housed near scarce or fragmented habitats, the additional pressure they exert can harm vulnerable species.

THE INDOOR CAT

One solution is simply to keep a cat indoors – although many owners claim that it's cruel. However, according to the Cats Indoors! campaign of the American Bird Conservancy there are many ways to make a cat happy with an indoor existence. For a start, plenty of toys and human interaction will keep a cat stimulated, but the local birds safe.

If you do want to allow a cat some outside space then you can construct or buy a suitable enclosure. While there is also a wide array of harnesses available that will allow you to take your cat for a walk, but keep it away from trouble. It's worth noting that there are even some places that have imposed legislation to prevent cats roaming free.

Even keeping a cat indoors just some of the time can make a big difference – especially during the spring and winter months – and the best times to do so are after bad weather and an hour after sunrise and before sunset.

THE OUTDOOR CAT

If keeping your cat indoors, or at least under control when out and about, isn't for you then there are still plenty of measures you can take.

To start with, cats are opportunistic hunters, so remove the source of the temptation by placing bird feed and bird feeders out of reach. Also, place bird boxes well away from any potential feline interference.

As well as considering where you place their food, you can give the birds more of a chance by planting shrubs that they can flee to – although you need to place these carefully to avoid them being used by cats as cover. Thorny plants or those with pungent odours will also deter cats from certain areas, or can be placed near feeders or fences to discourage cats from climbing them.

Finally, an RSPB report has shown the age-old bell on a collar to be an effective early warning system – reducing kills of both birds and small mammals by over a third. Although they do advise the use of quick-release collars, in case they become snagged.

A domestic cat may seem like gentle and docile pet, but it retains the genetics of a killing machine – at least as far as birds are concerned.

👀 GREAT BIRDWATCHING LITERATURE

Birdwatching in the form we could recognise today began in the late eighteenth century, and with this newfound passion came an explosion of literature about birds and everything related to birds. Since then many thousands of books have been published, and hundreds more are being written every year.

The following recommendations are just a few of the books I have particularly enjoyed over the years.

First up is *The Feather Quest: A North American Birder's Year* by Peter Dunne, who seems to be establishing himself as the successor to Roger Tory Peterson as the American face of knowledgeable birding. Similarly, his *Feather Quest* – which traces his seasonal birding travels – is something of a modern version of Peterson's 1935 *Wild America*. It's a wonderful blend of fact, folklore and philosophy, and very readable indeed.

Another tale of birding travels is Mark Obmascik's *The Big Year: A Tale of Man, Nature, and Fowl Obsession*. Take Hunter S. Thompson, replace the drugs with birds and you have something approaching this book. Obmascik follows the trail of three competitors through the course of the 1998 North American Big Year – a 365-day race across North America in search of the largest number of birds possible. The upshot is a highly entertaining and occasionally inspiring read.

The travels of birds themselves is the subject of *Living on the Wind: Across the Hemisphere With Migratory Birds*. Few can match Scott Weidensaul's exhaustive research, and the depth of information about migration in *Living on the Wind* is unbelievable.

Meanwhile, the *Atlas of Bird Migration: Tracing the Great Journeys of the World's Birds* lays claim to being the definitive work on the subject. Edited by Jonathan Elphick this impressive volume presents the work of an international corps of experts in a jargon-free style, creating a volume that should be on every birder's reference shelf, but which can also be read from cover to cover.

Remaining on the subject of bird behaviour, Marie Read's *Secret Lives of Common Birds: Enjoying Bird Behavior Through the Seasons* provides fascinating insights into everything from nest building to bathing. The science is there, but Read's lightness of touch makes this book accessible to a non-scientific audience. Moreover, her engaging writing style is coupled to her wonderful photography of birds and their behaviour.

Finally, *The Verb 'To Bird': Sightings of an Avid Birder* by Peter Cashwell makes for a fascinating journey in print. Part lexicography, part history, part travelogue and part popular commentary, *The Verb 'To Bird'* offers an entertaining look at the lore of birdwatching, and is an ideal place to start – once you've finished reading this of course.

🔭 COMPETITIVE BIRDWATCHING

In Europe it's called twitching, in the U.S. it's chasing. Regardless of the name we choose, it involves racing off to set eyes on the latest rare bird and tick it off our life-list. It's a specialised area of birdwatching, one that many have concerns about, but one that has nevertheless drawn large numbers of devotees.

When the first spotters of a golden-winged warbler in Kent, England decided not to 'suppress' the information about the location of the bird, more than 5,000 twitchers converged. Some of them 'dipped out' when they failed to see the bird and felt rather 'gripped off' towards those who did tick the bird off their lists. As you can see, twitching is specialised enough to have generated its own jargon.

THE NEXT STEP

It's not a big step from the already highly competitive world of twitching or chasing to the realm of organised competition. Consider the Big Year in the U.S. in which an individual has to record as many different bird species as he or she can over 365 days, often investing an incredible amount of time and money in the process.

Then there's the World Series of Birding each year, which uses the state of New Jersey as its playing field for 24 hours. There's even a finish line in that teams must turn in their totals by midnight at Cape May Lighthouse. The World Series has a charitable component and it also raises millions in pledges for various conservation organizations, but it is as hard-nosed as competition can be. Some teams spends weeks before the 24-hour event scouting New Jersey for every possible bird and then follow a predetermined plan for every moment of the event.

For the more competitive in our ranks, there are bird-spotting contests at nearly every level of ability and commitment, with the most taxing being the 365-day Big Year in the U.S.

It's not just birdwatching competitions that set people's pulses racing; there are also plenty of bird photography contests around the world open to amateurs and professionals alike – and these are a great way of improving your skills and perhaps getting to see your prize-winning shot in print.

As with so many other outdoor pursuits, our human nature has brought our competitive instincts to the world of birdwatching. Many of us are not convinced it's an unambiguously good thing. But that's not going to change a thing, and you can be sure that if there's something we can keep score of, we humans will almost inevitably make a sport of it.

📷 BIRD·PROOFING YOUR WINDOWS

No one has an accurate tally, but every year hundreds of thousands of birds around the world – perhaps even millions – are killed when they fly into windows. It's also likely that a similar number are injured or stunned and become easy prey for all sorts of animals, domestic and wild alike.

Birds clearly don't understand glass, and have trouble seeing it at the best of times. This is only too obvious from the frequency with which they thud into our windows, often when hurriedly fleeing a predator.

DECALS

Self-cling decals have been developed by several different companies as the solution to window strikes, and they are effective in most instances. Most clings are silhouettes of birds in flight and are available in white and black versions. They will stick to the inside or the outside of the window. Placing them outdoors improves their visibility regardless of the angle of the sun, but those on the inside will last longer.

The people behind a new decal, called WindowAlert, have taken the idea a

Attaching silhouettes to window panes is the most popular way of helping birds to avoid collision and injury.

step further. It is designed to reflect ultraviolet rays, and while the effect is invisible to human eyes, it's highly visible to birds.

At first you'll find that any clings will be instantly noticeable whenever you look through the window. However, give it a few days and eventually you will hardly notice they're there.

ALTERNATIVE SOLUTIONS

For those who are not too keen on sticking bird-shaped decals to their windows, simply closing the drapes, blinds or shades at the appropriate times of day can also solve the problem.

Changing the location of feeders, bird baths, nestboxes and the like is another approach to the problem. With just a bit of study it should become apparent from which of the possible launching spots the ill-fated flights are taking off. Sometimes all it takes is a small move to eliminate the troubling flight path. Shrubs and trees might also be the culprits.

Another option is to place bird-chasing items, like owl decoys, gigantic eyeballs, dangling strands of Mylar or other shimmering material, wind-spinners and the like, in front of or near the window that's the source of the collisions. Birds are pretty quick to avoid any area where they sense a threat, even a threat they don't completely understand.

ᨎ HAND·FEEDING WILD BIRDS

To me hand-feeding a wild bird runs counter to many ideas about birdwatching. And beyond the world of birding it conjures images of dangerous and sometimes deadly situations when wild animals become overly familiar with humans and, moreover, associate us with food. Of course those concerns generally focus on bigger, more dangerous creatures like bears, and some of our fellows want to give hand-feeding of birds a try – a few even make an art out of it – so we will discuss it here.

If as a kid you generally won the game of statues, you just might have the temperament needed for hand-feeding. While this aspect of birdwatching doesn't require the participant to be abused like those guano-covered statues in the park, the ability to remain still is certainly an essential skill.

Training wild birds to accept seed from a human's hand is an exercise in patience and persistence that will pay off only with particular species.

ESTABLISH A ROUTINE

First, establish a regular routine for your garden birds. Fill the feeders at the same time each morning or afternoon. Make some soft, but unique sound every time you are filling the feeders, not something that will scare off the birds, but something that will call their attention to your feeding schedule. Place some treats – out-of-the-shell sunflower kernels, walnut meats or suet – in the area where you plan to attempt the hand-feeding. Maintain this routine every day for several weeks.

When it's obvious the birds know your schedule, continue with your daily routine, but sit still about half a dozen paces from where you placed the treats. Wearing similar colours every day, do this until the birds have come with you sitting there for several days in a row.

After the birds learn to tolerate your presence, begin moving your chair just a little closer each day. Then run through your daily routine and sit with your cupped hand filled with the treats. Remain motionless and in position.

By this point, some of the birds should be ready to take the treats from your palm. You will most likely notice that it's only some individuals that are willing to take this risk. Spend several weeks at this stage, then eventually you may be able to move gradually away from the feeding area and still have those birds coming to you for their treats.

Finally, begin talking softly, but in your normal voice, to the birds that feed from your hand. If you're lucky and patient enough you might get to the stage where you can step out into the back garden and call your favourites to come and feed from your hand.

📋 COMING TO TERMS WITH FEATHERED PREDATORS

As we've already discussed with cats, the presence of large numbers of birds at your feeders is going to attract the attention of predators, just as any concentration of prey species would in the wild. And some of those predators will be feathered just like their prey. Hawks eat birds, and some hawks even specialise in avian prey. So, wherever small birds gather hawks will eventually show up and begin making their diving attacks.

Songbirds, being prey species, know they are vulnerable to hawks and will keep a careful watch on the skies. Among the numerous benefits of flocking is the ability to have many pairs of eyes constantly on watch for predators, both airborne and terrestrial. In fact, they're most likely to spot a threat before you do, so take your cue from them; when all the birds at the feeder suddenly freeze or dart off into the shrubbery, look to the sky for the hawk.

Compounding the problem – for the hawk at least – is the reality that it will see no reward for most of its attacks. There's a reason for the fact that hawks spend so much time hovering overhead, weighing up the opportunities below until they finally settle on odds that make their efforts worthwhile.

The bottom line is this: A hawk will actually take very few birds at any given feeding station. However, being the sentimental creatures that we are, humans often feel the need to do something about such a situation that doesn't suit our sensibilities. It doesn't matter that there is very little we can do, short of surrender to the vagaries of nature.

Many who feed birds in their gardens set the table for small, prey species and then resent predators, such as hawks, when they too come to the buffet.

WHAT CAN YOU DO?

If you really don't feel that you can let nature take its course then be aware that taking any direct action, even with just the intention of 'scaring off' the hawk is not acceptable. Laws at all levels protect hawks from attack, often even any disturbance, from humans. Even if you do it with the intention of protecting other birds you run a real risk of harming the 'offending' bird, and would you really want to, even if it were within the law? You're a birdwatcher, right?

Having ruled out the option of fighting back, the most effective option is to eliminate the attraction for the hawk. If you stop feeding for a week or two then the songbirds will disperse, and this in turn removes the source of the hawk's temptation. Soon the predator will eliminate your backyard from its hunting territory, at which time you can reinstate your feeding. Be advised, though, that this is unlikely to be anything other than a temporary fix, and a hawk – perhaps the same one, perhaps not – will probably show up again. Whereupon you will have to repeat the whole process.

Another, more permanent fix, but also one that will generally see less immediate impact on the predator–prey interactions, is that of planting evergreen shrubs and trees close enough to provide some cover into which the feeding birds can escape. However, if you do choose this route, it's important to place the shrubs at the right distance. Too far away and they will be of little help to the fleeing birds; too close and they can provide effective cover for stalking terrestrial predators such as cats.

NATURE'S COURSE
The final option is the easiest, the most environmentally aware and ultimately maybe the most enjoyable. Why not accept the hawk as a natural part of the ecosystem? Just one more bird your feeding station is attracting, and a fairly unusual and interesting one at that. Give the songbirds a fighting chance with some cover, then sit back and enjoy the show.

Help Bird Conservation

A new phase of conservation work has been sweeping the birdwatching community. Known as 'citizen science', it has opened a range of possibilities for non-scientist volunteers to contribute far beyond the simple donation of funds. Through organisations such as Audubon and the Cornell Laboratory of Ornithology we average, everyday enthusiasts can make real contributions to scientific inquiry.

Our observations have value, especially when directed into specific areas of inquiry, specific research projects. We can give the researchers the data points for their work. We can expand the data they have at their disposal to make their research more comprehensive, more definitive.

It's not an excuse for passing on the chance to also donate cold, hard cash, but it is an opportunity for further involvement, and that can be the basis for real change and action.

These days anyone can contribute their observations to research databases.

🔭 PLANNING THE CLUB OUTING

If it can go wrong, it will, and usually during the outing you're running for the birding club. The best advice is to follow the Scouts' maxim and 'be prepared'.

For most short outings that means carrying a penknife, duct tape, a length of cord, a first-aid kit, a compass, good maps, a phone or radio and some extra water. However, its best to make sure you don't have to rely on this kit by planning in advance. This will also ensure a much more enjoyable outing for everyone involved.

THE GROUP
Start with group size – when you allow a birding group to grow larger than a half-dozen or so, you've slipped into planning a hike rather than a birdwatching outing. A smaller group encourages more openness and sharing of information between experienced birders and beginners. It also makes for much quieter, and less intrusive travel, which almost always means sighting more birds close-up.

Guides who are expert, both in birding and the local area, almost always enhance the experience. And as the leader it's up to you to recognise when your own knowledge falls short of the mark.

OTHER CONSIDERATIONS
The more details of the outing that can be anticipated and planned for, the fewer unpleasant surprises will lie in wait for you. Take some advice from

The world of birdwatching, and birding groups in particular, offers some wonderful opportunities for camaraderie.

jolly Old St Nick and check your list twice, at least. Acquiring a depth of knowledge as regards the terrain, water sources and weather conditions likely to be encountered is as much a part of your job as knowing about the birds you might see.

And, now that you have everything planned, down to fine details, allow for some flexibility. Levels of ability, fitness, preparedness and so on will vary widely among members – a fact you should be especially aware of with those with whom you never ventured forth before. A flexible attitude will make the experience more enjoyable for everyone, not least you.

🔭 GROUP WATCHES WITH KIDS

Involving children in birdwatching at an early age is a great way of helping them to develop an interest in the natural world. Taking them along on a normal group birdwatching excursion with grown-ups might not be such a great idea, as they will inevitably enjoy a different type of experience from that which is best suited to adults.

A group of children of varying ages will most likely present a far wider range of challenges than an equivalent number of adults. Therefore it is crucial that you have enough responsible adults available to meet each child's needs. If you're planning a birthday party, or similar excursion with quite a few kids, then that can mean inviting parents along to help out.

It's worth putting in a great deal of thought when it comes to the destination of the trip, and organised birding centres are an excellent option. Not only do they tend to offer a lot of good birding opportunities in a relatively compact area, but many even provide child-friendly activity programmes, and offer a range of other activities for when the kids begin to tire.

BIRDING MATTERS

Lights, Cameras, Action...

I remember the day, and it doesn't seem all that long ago, when getting a good photo of a bird meant lugging a backpack's worth of gear around with you. Then, when your luck wasn't in, you'd have to lug it all back home again without so much as a snapshot for your troubles.

Today many digital cameras of all levels offer enough technological wizardry to grab a decent image. Sure, the pros still carry a great deal of gear to get their magazine covers – and there's nothing stopping you doing the same if you're more ambitious – but the rest of us are now perfectly well catered for by digital compacts.

This ease of use and cost-free shooting means that the risk of a duff shot is no longer stopping people from taking a camera birdwatching. So what if only one shot in a hundred is any good; just delete the rest – they haven't cost you anything!

If you do want to brush up on your technique, then there are a few basic tips on p. 32; but please, whatever your level of ability, just get shooting. And not just birds. Why not take some photos of your birding buddies, or the landscape, or a beautiful sunset – after all, it's free.

👀 PASSING ON THE TRADITION

'Dad. Quick, come here. What's that bird?' My kid is simply hooked on birds! He's also hooked on pretty much anything else related to the great outdoors, which, in my book, is just perfect.

Spending time together is the basis for getting a child involved in any hobby. However, exactly where you spend that time is probably not so important, and in the context of birdwatching, there really is no better starting point than your backyard or the nearest park.

Excursions into the countryside can be grand adventures, but they also involve all that boring travelling time, and are probably best saved until after your kids have first enjoyed their own backyard experience.

Also, you'll want to plan and carry out your birdwatching at a time of day when the most birds of the greatest variety will be present. In most of our gardens, that's early morning or late afternoon into early evening.

Children generally thrill to the chase of birdwatching and especially enjoy the small victories of spotting and identifying birds.

KITTING OUT YOUR KID
Hand the child his or her own binoculars as you begin the outing and you've pretty much sealed the deal. As far as the specifics go, they do not need to carry a hefty price tag; a basic pair of binoculars with reasonable optics is just fine for starters. There are those models designed and decorated just for children, but maybe this is a good time to give the child a taste of adulthood, of admittance to something special, beyond the world of kids. Just make sure they are easy to focus and offer a wide enough field of view to make aiming them easier.

When it comes to field guides, beginners' or children's versions are now available from a variety of publishers for nearly every location, and the prices are generally reasonable.

Make sure the child is dressed in appropriate clothes, and a number of layers will help regulate temperature in the field. Comfortable headgear and sunglasses may also be required. And, when it comes to comfort, don't forget the insect repellent!

IN THE FIELD
Explain to the child that more birds will reveal themselves if the two of you move slowly and quietly, and take some time to

just sit still at regular intervals. Small, light field stools will make this aspect of the outing more comfortable.

When you spot a bird, try to wait until the child tells you it is there. Boost the child's sense of accomplishment by allowing him or her to describe the key identifying features such as the bird's colours, its size and its beak, along with any calls or interesting behaviour. You might even want to take a notebook with you, allowing the child to make notes and sketches if he or she wants to take on that responsibility.

Keep the outing to a reasonable length of time, and keep tabs on just how well the child's attention span is holding up.

BACK HOME

While there's nothing wrong with celebrating your findings in the field – quietly of course – the best time for this is when you get back home. This gives you the chance to pull out a more sophisticated field guide and share additional information about the birds you've just seen. You can also check the internet for sites where you can post a report or photograph of your sightings.

If you get it right – and you're careful not to exhaust your child's patience – you can spark a lifelong interest. Over the months and years you can extend the length of the trips, camping out and taking in some real adventures that you can enjoy together.

Common-Sense Courtesy

He had been lying behind the log at the side of the trail, watching the small flock of wild turkeys, for a quarter of an hour or so, just him and the beautiful birds that didn't have a clue he was there. The turkeys leisurely scratched in the leaves, plucking up and swallowing any acorns they uncovered.

Suddenly every turkey's head popped up and turned to gaze down the trail, not at the concealed man who had been watching them, but at a couple strolling towards them. The pair were gesturing at the birds, which were by now turning to flee, and signalling the man to look at the birds, which he was clearly already doing. He held up a hand to signal them to stop. They didn't understand. They walked right up to him, watching the turkeys disappear over the next ridge, and whooped about what they had just seen, expecting him to share their glee.

Stumbling across others in the outdoors and disturbing their activities is inevitable. But being aware of what is going on around you is the common-sense route to sharing our dwindling outdoor spaces with the others who use them as well.

🔭 MAKING SENSE OF BIRD SENSES

Never handle a baby bird because the parents will then reject it. Balderdash! There are plenty of good reasons not to handle a baby bird, but this isn't one of them – most birds have a relatively weak sense of smell. The popular understanding of birds' other senses is equally sketchy, so lets take a closer look.

There are exceptions to most species' poor olfactory sense. Smell plays a part in helping vultures find their carcass du jour, but it is not crucial as experiments have shown that covering a carcass from view presents vultures with problems, while they will also attempt to eat a picture of a sheep carcass.

Similarly, petrels and albatrosses use scent to locate blood and meat spread across the surface of the ocean, while experiments show petrels can and do locate their nests by smell.

SIGHT AND SOUND

For most birds, vision is the critical sense. Just consider the relative size of the avian eye. An owl's eyes – which are champion light-gathering devices – contribute a third of its head's total weight. Even in birds like the starling, the eyes account for more than a tenth of the head weight. In contrast, your eyes are only about a hundredth of the weight of your head.

It's hardly surprising that legends have grown around the perceived eyesight of birds, and indeed hawks do see two or three times more sharply than humans. However, this is not true of all birds, and studies of the structure of vultures' eyes indicate that they are little better than human eyes, while the vision of domestic chickens is downright myopic.

When it comes to sound, birds hear the middle frequencies about as well as mammals, although they're not as sensitive to high and low frequencies. On the other hand, birds are many times more sensitive to quick changes in the pitch and intensity of sounds.

Birds do not have the external apparatus of ears like those of mammals. Instead, most have special feathers around their ear openings that cut air movement across their auditory sensors, like wind screens do for microphones. Owls, which have some of the most acute hearing on the planet, can even reposition the feathers around their ear openings to the extent of being able to

Owls have some of the most acute hearing on any creatures, enhanced with the ability to reposition feathers and widely rotate their heads to better pick up sounds.

Hummingbird beaks and tongues are elongated out of proportion to the rest of the bird's body, enabling the hummers to feed from deep, trumpet-shaped flowers.

shape them into a bowl similar to the human ear.

It's also interesting to note that it isn't just bats that employ echolocation; for example, penguins use it to find prey, while oilbirds navigate using it.

TASTE AND TOUCH

Birds generally have fewer taste buds than mammals, indicating that their sense of taste is generally less capable of differentiation. As always, however, there are exceptions, such as hummingbirds that are able to distinguish between different sugar concentrations in nectar from different flowers.

Like the other senses, the sense of touch in birds is also nowhere near fully understood, but the placement of nerve endings in the skin indicates that it is a fairly acute sense. There are also concentrations of those nerve endings in critical spots, such as the tip of a goose's bill, which is used to probe for food.

Some species of birds even have whiskers, like those of a cat, around their beaks. These 'rictal' bristles have clusters of nerve cells at their bases, and species that snatch and eat insects on the wing, such as swallows and flycatchers, make particularly good use of them.

But, even without rictal bristles, all birds feel through their feathers. Of course, like human hair, feathers are not living material, but are held in place by follicles that house nerve endings. When the feather touches something, even just an air current, a sensation is passed along to the bird's central nervous system.

So there is our brief summary of avian senses. Although there are many common features, what makes sense such an interesting subject is the impact it has on variety – as is also the case with avian evolution and anatomy (see p. 14 and p. 18).

A great deal of the diversity of birds and bird behaviour is attributable to the different uses of their senses – their strengths and weaknesses. And it is this diversity that makes birds such a fascinating subject.

👓 THINGS THAT GO BUMP IN THE NIGHT

We've all been out birding after dark – whether waiting for a night-flying species or simply leaving it a little late to make it back in daylight. Likewise, we all know the spine-tingling sensation of being watched and the eerie silence that causes us to quicken our step, hastening for the warmth of home.

Spare a thought, then, for the poor snipe hunter – the naive victim of a popular prank. The stooge is handed a sack and a flashlight, and led to a clearing in the forest. There they must lay in wait for the elusive snipe, holding the sack open and shining the flashlight into it – snipes apparently like their hiding places well lit. The pranksters then disappear into the forest to drive the snipes in the sacker's direction, although they are secretly returning to camp.

The test is how long the lonely snipe hunter will bear the darkness, growing ever more nervous in the dead of night. The natural sounds of the forest, many of them birds – perhaps even a snipe – provide the spooky soundtrack.

The irony of the snipe hunt is that there really is a bird called a snipe – just not one that nests in a sack.

👓 REAR-WINDOW BIRDWATCHING

Backyards across the globe are the site of far more birdwatching than any exotic location or bird preserve. It's a simple matter of proximity – we spend more time in our gardens and at the windows in our homes overlooking our backyards – so it's only natural that the bulk of our birdwatching should be done there.

Bird researchers and organisations have not missed the fact that a great deal has been learned by watching birds in gardens across the globe. Bird-feeding studies and population surveys are now relying on the huge corps of citizen scientists and what they discover right outside their rear windows.

If you're not already involved, then there's no reason not to be. In North America there's the annual Great Backyard Bird Count, while in Britain there's the Big Garden BirdWatch to mention but two examples. These studies tap into all that backyard bird knowledge and experience; what's more they're a good way of becoming more involved in the birding community – so give it a go, they're great fun!

🔭 GPS AND BIRDWATCHING

As we've already seen, modern technologies have changed the face of birding – arguably none more so than the Global Positioning System (GPS). With a GPS unit in hand, the exact location where a bird has been spotted can be pinpointed, recorded and shared in an instant. However, while the technology offers doubtless potential benefits, it also poses potential pitfalls – it all depends on how you use it.

Among the advantages of GPS is the precision of its information. This helps birders to return to the exact same location time after time, which is ideal for recording long-term population variations. It also allows other birders to make their way to the same spot and confirm previous sightings, or otherwise collaborate over a period of time.

In addition, GPS units can often prove invaluable when it comes to finding your way. Many offer a great degree of interaction and the ability to log landmarks, routes and waypoints at home on your computer before taking them into the field – an especially helpful feature for those who journey off the beaten path in their pursuit of birds. Furthermore, many people find these relatively new gadgets easier to get to grips with than the traditional skills of using a map and compass.

It's also interesting to note that bird researchers have recognised the value inherent in GPS and often attach small transmitters to the birds they are studying. This is much less costly and time intensive than the telemetry systems previously available – and some of the results are available online.

The Flipside

As always there are downsides, one of which is that the increased precision and ease of sharing data can overload vulnerable locations with birders.

However, it is hard to fault the technology itself – as always, it's a case of what you do with it that counts.

Global Positioning System technology allows people to find very precise locations anywhere on the face of the Earth, including prime birdwatching spots.

![binoculars] ARE MAPS STILL RELEVANT?

Having looked at the technical advances offered by GPS units, it would be tempting to assume that traditional topographic maps were no longer relevant. However, they do still have an important role to play, and not just when your GPS unit runs out of batteries.

A map isn't just a useful backup to a more-sophisticated piece of kit. If you choose the right scale, it provides sweeping views of the landscape, but with enough detail to enable you to locate likely spots for good birding.

The crux of the matter is understanding the relationship between birds and their preferred habitats, and the likelihood that a specific geographical feature will offer that habitat.

For example, many species of birds hone in on forested wetlands. A topographic map will reveal the locations of wetlands, the general type of landscape cover across the site and the presence of any buildings and roads that a birder might use to access the spot.

KEEPING TRACK

Paper maps also serve as a fine record-keeping tool for bird sightings, and for that matter whatever else you discover on your outings. You can build up a map in this way over the passing seasons and years, creating an increasingly useful and personalised tool.

Furthermore, it's worth noting that maps themselves haven't escaped the march of technology, and you can have one printed specifically for your requirements. Some also interface with GPS units to add the user's discoveries at the exact coordinates.

In essence, electronic kit is best used not as a replacement for a paper map, but as an enhancement of it. What's more,

for those of us that grew up with them at least, there's an undeniable appeal to the old skills of map and compass – that is when we don't get lost.

Despite technological developments in the form of GPS units and the like, maps remain a relevant, and often more enjoyable tool for birdwatchers.

🔭 THE MOST BEAUTIFUL BIRDS

Those who are lucky and dedicated enough to travel the world in search of new birdwatching experiences often list the brilliantly coloured, magnificently plumed quetzals of the New World tropics as the most beautiful birds they've ever seen. The shimmering plumage, the jungle setting, what's not to love?

The quetzal may even be the longest-standing contender for the title of most beautiful bird. Since ancient times the indigenous peoples of the region – the Maya, the Aztecs and others – revered the bird as a symbol of beauty. The modern name is derived from *quetzalli*, which was used mostly to describe the beautiful tail feathers by the Aztecs, who believed the bird was so beautiful that to cage it would kill it.

Many consider the brilliant plumage of the quetzal to be the most beautiful among all birds.

PERSONAL PREFERENCE

However, 'most beautiful' is a subjective term at best, packed with personal preferences and unique experiences. The male ring-necked pheasant is a shimmering specimen in its own right, particularly in the right sunlight. The soaring bald eagle is majestically beautiful. The indigo bunting touches brilliant blues you could never have imagined. The beautiful peafowl has been spread to the four corners of the globe by people who valued the male's wondrous, metallic tail eyes. And then there is the turkey vulture, which in the right light and … well, maybe not the turkey vulture.

It's difficult to run through any list of birds and not find something rather attractive about each species. Even the lowly house sparrow has those lovely chestnut tones.

So, on a rainy afternoon, why not make your own list, and ask your friends and family to make theirs as well. Start with those birds you've actually seen in the wild, then expand upon that to a wish-list of those that you've yet to see. You'll tend to find that different people's lists have little in common, and provide hours of lively debate, whether face to face or online.

👓 KEEPING A JOURNAL

Even before the term birdwatching was coined, birdwatchers were maintaining their birdwatching journals. Indeed, some of the earliest birdwatching books were simply a matter of publishing the edited journals of a particularly dedicated birder.

Today there is little chance that even the best-kept of our journals will ever become a book. However, journal-keeping remains central to the essence of being a birdwatcher. Indeed, it is sometimes said that a nature journal kept in the field – rather than any education, training or experience – is the difference between someone who simply enjoys nature and a true naturalist. Such a journal is at once the ongoing, developing memory of the birdwatcher and also an ever more advanced, educational primer provided by their own observations.

START AT THE BEGINNING

A journal begins as a simple blank notebook and can become as simple or as complicated as its owner desires. At the very least a journal will record the date, time, temperature, weather conditions and location for each entry, the type of bird observed, and a few notes on its behaviour and song. If you want to take it a little further, then many birders create an address-book-cum-travel guide with the names and details of new contacts, and notes on any accommodation used.

For the artistically minded, sketches in the margin – or, if you'd like, more centrally – can make the journal even more attractive and useful. And it is all the more meaningful if it is done while in the field.

To evolve your journal to the next level entails the compilation of an index of entries. This can be a separate volume – preparing it on computer makes it more easily editable – that lists the major recurring subjects in your journals, such as species of birds and locations, and the volume and page of the journal on which they can be found. Although this might take a little extra time, it will doubtless give you greater insight over the course of a few seasons.

HOW TO WRITE

Plenty of people have difficulty getting started, so a good style of writing is 'stream of consciousness'. Rather than pausing to think about each entry, just write it as it comes to mind. Journals are personal, so don't waste time trying to find the perfect turn of phrase when it's unlikely that anyone else will read it. However, if you like, you can always pass them on for another generation to continue.

KEEPING GOING

It's important that keeping your journal doesn't become a chore, otherwise the day will soon come when you put it to one side, never to pick it up again.

Don't worry about keeping an entry for every day just keep as few or as many notes as you desire – after all, an infrequent journal is better than none at all. With that in mind, many journalists choose to keep their current notebooks close at hand, or near the window in their home from which they most often watch birds. Thereby, when the opportunity presents itself, you can pen a few quick lines, make a sketch and have done with it.

Some have suggested that the new generation of ultra-small digital camcorders might serve as the new medium of journal-keeping. But, for me, a simple documentation of what is seen does not a journal make.

Although some journals have become popular books, most represent a very personal record for the individual birdwatcher.

THAT FIRST BIRD

Pause for a second and think back to the first bird you can remember seeing. Recall as much as you can. Such first-bird memories, at least when they involve identification, usually involve the guidance of some older member of the family.

My personal first is one such example. My late mother did most of her birdwatching through her kitchen window, and it was this vantage point that provided my first taste of birding. I think it was a mockingbird that each year nested in the barberry hedge along the edge of our backyard, or perhaps an evening grosbeak on a wintertime irruption south to better feeding grounds, or one of the pheasants that roamed the fields just beyond our hedge.

It's hard to tell which came first now, but they're vivid memories nonetheless, and they take me right back.

Remember your first bird? I can, and it takes me right back.

BIRDING BUDDIES

As the small birdwatching party I was leading emerged from the forest into the parking lot, I noticed a somewhat familiar face in another group that was just arriving and preparing to move out. She seemed to return my confused stare, apparently working through the same questions in her mind: Do I know that person? Where have I met him before? The answers seemed to come to us both at about the same time, judging from the smiles that spread across our faces at almost the same instant.

Then we were both off for the middle of the parking lot, throwing our arms around each other. Years earlier we had both been part of a birdwatching group led by a mutual friend in Yellowstone National Park. Today, the two of us were standing at the edge of a forest mountain in eastern Pennsylvania, about two-thirds of a continent east of where we met.

We had kept in touch, first by letter and then by e-mail, sharing many tales of our birding exploits and often wondering if we would ever bird together again. Now we were almost doing just that. My group was finishing up, hers was just starting out. But we were both going to be in the same area at least another day and would alter our plans for tomorrow so that we could get out together.

Birding relationships can be like that. Years may pass between shared experiences; however, the common ground of spotting and studying new birds is always there as a tie that binds. There is always something new to share, and when the opportunity arises to once again get in some birding time together it is snatched up and cherished. And it's often as if very little time has passed.

The mother of another birding friend died recently. It had been decades since we last corresponded in any way. But

The birdwatching world can be amazingly small, with old acquaintances surfacing in the most unexpected of places.

in his response to my initial e-mail of condolence, he recalled a happier time on a lake in wilderness Quebec and the divers (or loons) we enjoyed so much together. I hope the memory lifted his spirits just a little.

Other birdwatching friends remain closer at hand and ready for regular excursions in the shared pursuit of new birds or new knowledge about old birds. Attendance at the same bird club meetings and chance meetings in the same outdoor spots again and again forge and maintain the connections.

ONLINE BUDDIES

And today we have the world of the internet. The word 'friend' has taken on an entirely new digital meaning. No longer are we required to have met someone face to face before calling them friend. Photos of birding accomplishments and discoveries are shared with the click of a mouse. In the world of chatroom pseudonyms, you never know, you might live next door to the person you're talking to, having never shared a birdwatching conversation face to face but having become hard-and-fast buddies in the virtual world.

Birding is a solid foundation for many friendships. It gives you plenty to talk about, a focus for your friendship, and also that edge of competitiveness mixed with a collaborative spirit that you get when like-minded people are pursuing the same goal. And, thankfully, it seems to me that all of these values continue to thrive within birdwatching communities whether online or, as I still prefer it, with your boots on the ground.

Leave No Trace

As a birdwatcher you have no excuse not to minimise your impact on the environment. Here are the rules, plain and simple:

+ Plan ahead to maximise your enjoyment and safety and minimise your environmental impacts.
+ Concentrate or spread your activity according to the site. In areas of already high impact, concentrated activities will do less additional harm. In remote, wild areas with low previous impact, spreading out an activity will minimise your impact.
+ If you take it with you, take it home again.
+ Dispose of bodily waste properly.
+ Dispose of all wastewater at least 200 ft (60 m) from any water.
+ Take only photos and recordings. Leave everything the way you found it. Minimise alterations to the site.
+ Minimise campfire use.
+ Respect the wildlife and observe it from a distance that causes no stress.
+ Respect other people by travelling in small groups, keeping the noise down, avoiding sites already under use, wearing colours that blend with the environment (except during hunting seasons), staying out of private property and leaving gates how you found them.

🔭 YOUR LIFE-LIST

Serious birdwatchers take their life-lists seriously. After all, life-lists are the chronicles of their lives as birders – accounts of every species they have seen. The search for that elusive bird to fill out a gap in the list never ends and can lead individual birdwatchers to extremes of effort, travel and expense.

The life-lists of most casual birdwatchers usually stand at about 300 species. If a birder managed to see every species of bird in North America, a life-list would total about 850; in the United Kingdom, about 500; and worldwide, around 10,000.

A life-list can be maintained in any way the birder wants. However, the most useful order will be phylogenetic, which uses Latin names (see p. 17) with the overall list divided by order, then family, genus and finally species. Ordering the birds like this makes such a list more navigable.

A WORD OF WARNING
A life list can be a great aide-memoire, but avoid the trap that many birders fall into – don't make your list the sole focus of your efforts. Yes, it's great to see a bird you've waited for years to encounter, and it can be satisfying to add it to your list. But when all's said and done, you're not going to see all of the birds in the world; so why not enjoy the ones that you do meet, and don't fret so much about those you've missed.

🔭 THE TRUTH OF THE MATTER

Here, near the middle of this little volume, I thought would be the perfect place to share the central secret of birdwatching. It's a hobby, a pursuit, maybe a passion, perhaps a sport; but, for most of us at least, it is neither a science nor a profession.

Some of us might be contributing our observations to this or that scientific study, or perhaps taking part in a competition of sorts. But the bottom line remains that we are chasing through field and forest after tiny singing bundles of feathers.

It's great that the vast majority of us have a deep concern for the growing environmental threats to the birds and all of nature; it is after all a serious subject. But at the same time, it's important that we don't take ourselves too seriously.

Of course it's nice to share our observations and sightings, but all too often we serve them up as though at the altar of some religion. A genuine passion for our hobby is fascinating, but too deep an intensity can be trying in the extreme.

Take a breath, think back to the reason you started watching birds – and if you feel yourself teetering close to the brink of obsessiveness then tone it down a bit.

👓 BAGS AND VESTS

Having the right gear to hand, and in good working order, can make or break a birding trip. We cover specific items in many of the other entries, but here we shall examine the means we use to carry all that kit into the field – with any luck dry and in one piece.

The main choice for most birdwatchers is between vests and bags. With so many models on the market, I'll avoid making specific recommendations. Instead here are a few general pointers to look for.

VESTS

Vests are popular among birdwatchers. They boast lots of pockets of different sizes – which should close securely to keep gear from spilling out, as it so often does when you stop to tie a lace. Spreading your kit around the various pockets distributes its weight, but comfortable padding for the shoulders, chest and back is still essential. Finally, the waterproofing should be good enough to protect your stuff.

BAGS

Alternatively, many people use a bag in place of a vest. There are similar considerations as vests when it comes to waterproofing, and convenient pockets for ease of access. But a bag will alter the way a load is carried, and for this reason it's wise to invest in one with a decent system of harnesses that you can adjust to protect your back.

Birdwatchers never seem to have enough pockets or space in their backpack, regardless of the vests and bags they strap onto themselves. Reducing the gear we carry never seems to come into question.

NESTBOXES

Installing and properly maintaining nestboxes can have a more direct benefit for birds than any other single thing a homeowner will ever do. Nestboxes can even have a real impact on the population of what are known as 'cavity nesters', many of which are in great need of a helping hand due in large part to the felling of old trees that offer such cavities.

The terms 'cavity tree' and 'den tree' commonly refer to a tree that is partially hollow and has holes leading from that hollow to the outside world, making the cavity useful to birds. Natural processes can take a half-century or longer to develop a proper cavity, which we humans can then destroy in moments. The decline of cavities correlates fairly directly with the decline of cavity-nesting birds, such as bluebirds, woodpeckers and kestrels.

In some places the competition for cavities is so fierce that every available nestbox will be eagerly snatched up. However, as coveted as every cavity may be, not every cavity or nestbox is suitable for every species of cavity-nester. Certainly, most nestboxes look similar, consisting of four walls, one with an entrance hole, a roof and a floor. But if you leave it at that you'll likely find starlings taking over the box every time.

The Right Kind of Home

The diameter of the entrance hole is among the most critical of nestbox measurements. Birds are looking for a secure site, and that means somewhere that they can access easily, but that other species might find trickier.

Along with the various design and size preferences among the different bird species, there also are concerns with location. In short, the most well-built, properly designed and elaborately

equipped nestbox will not attract the desired species if it's placed in the wrong environment. For example, kestrels prefer their cavities at the edge of fields with scattered trees, while robins, swallows and finches prefer large fields with

Cavity-nesting birds have benefitted greatly from the urge of backyard birdwatchers to erect nestboxes as additional encouragements for the birds to make their backyards into their homes.

scattered large trees, and nuthatches, titmice, chickadees and wrens prefer the forest interior.

THE IMPORTANCE OF MAINTENANCE

For this next section, I must admit, I am asking you to do as I say rather than as I do. That confession made, proper maintenance of nestboxes is essential to their continued benefit to birds. Other creatures, like squirrels, mice, bees and wasps are certain to try to move in and sometimes need to be forcibly evicted. Unwanted species like starlings and sparrows will often try to be the first to occupy the nestbox – and nesting material should be removed before any nest takes form. And, after each use by the birds, the nestbox should be cleaned to fight the spread of disease and pests.

I have never been very good about this maintenance end of the business. I generally allow the birds to use a nestbox until it falls apart. Then I have my son, who is handy at that type of thing, build a replacement. It's not as things should be, but it always seems to work out that way. One such neglected nestbox exploded over the course of a few months, as its tired old nails gave way to its constant stuffing with nesting materials by a particularly ambitious squirrel.

Dos and Don'ts of Nestboxes

+ Do use the right size and design for the bird you want to benefit.
+ Do protect nestboxes from cats and other predators by placing them away from shrubs and closely overhanging tree branches, and equip the supporting post with a baffle or predator band.
+ Do drill a few ventilation holes in the side of the nestbox and some drainage holes in the floor.
+ Do have the inside surface of the side of the nestbox leading from the floor to the entrance hole to help baby birds make their debut.
+ Do have one side of the nestbox hinged for ease of cleaning.

+ Don't use a metal nestbox. It will not provide the insulation needed by the youngsters inside.
+ Don't add a perch in front of the nestbox entrance hole, as it will attract other birds to harass the occupants or worse.
+ Don't hang a nestbox as it too easily could fall, injuring the occupants.
+ Don't paint the inside of a nestbox, as the chemicals in the paint will interfere with the natural cooling and warming of the wood and with it the interior of the nestbox.

THINK WATER

Water is a magnet for birds. It's not nearly so easily available in the wild as we tend to assume – especially when there's been a dry spell. But even when conditions are not so desperate, the availability of water will greatly increase the drawing power of your garden.

While drinking water is a critical need for wildlife, creatures are also drawn to it for other reasons. Bathing is one such example, and many backyard birds seem to relish water for just that purpose, sometimes spending long periods dousing themselves, perching nearby to preen and then returning to the water. Birds bathe for many reasons: to remove dirt and parasites from their feathers is one of the most obvious. However, a good splash can also help cool the bird down on a hot day.

If you have no existing water source on or near your garden, simply placing a bird bath there (see p. 83), and keeping it clean and filled with fresh water, will attract many more birds, and in far greater variety, than you now have. That's guaranteed – install it and they will come.

Moving Water

Any water feature in the backyard can be transformed from bird magnet to super-magnet by adding the sound of moving water. You don't have to splash out on an elaborate and pricey waterfall array – simply punch a few tiny holes in the bottom of a plastic bottle, such as a large milk carton, and suspend it above your bird bath or pond. The sound will travel and attract birds from a considerable distance around.

Ground-level water sources, ranging from simple pans placed on the lawn and kept filled with water, to large and extensive ponds, are the big time of backyard water features. They take your garden to the next level, aquatically speaking. The larger and more diversified the water source, the greater the variety of birds, and other wildlife, it will attract.

Whatever ground-level or in-ground water source your interest, time and budget will permit, a variety of depths optimises the usefulness of the water source to birds and all wildlife. In a simple arrangement intended only to provide bathing opportunity for birds, the depths should vary from a ½-in (1¼ cm) to no more than 3 in (7½ cm), although a maximum depth of 2 in (5 cm) is best.

The structure itself should offer enough flat areas with slightly rough, non-slippery surfaces. At the other end of the spectrum, a water source intended to attract and hold aquatic life should range from ½ in (1¼ cm) to at least 2 ft (60 cm) at the centre, which is sufficient to keep at least some of the water from freezing during winter in most of the temperate regions of the world. Adding a water pump also works to this end during the cold months.

Adding a water source of such depth to your garden may need permission of some sort from a local authority. Even if it doesn't require any official authorisation, you would do well to consider any safety concerns that would arise with the installation of a pond, especially where children are concerned.

The addition of running water to your garden will attract a great many more birds.

RECYCLING

Many backyard 'birdscapers' have used recycled materials, ranging from home bathtubs to old metal drums cut in half, as the foundation for their water features. However, such arrangements are of limited usefulness to birds.

With that in mind, they can easily be made more useful and attractive to birds by adding rocks and other elements to vary their depths, eliminate slippery surfaces and provide underwater attraction for insect life. For example, an old bathtub sunk into the ground and refurbished in this manner, perhaps with a few potted water plants, will quickly lose its unnatural appearance and be given a truly functional second life.

There is a strong creative aspect to using such materials in making a mini-pond or similar feature. And it can be deeply satisfying to make something of your own in this way. What's more, it is a great way of creating a positive environmental impact from something that otherwise just be taking up space in a landfill site.

BUYING NEW

The benefits of recycling aside, most people choose to invest in a new pond, if their budget allows it. These tend to take the form of ready-made, premoulded plastic mini-ponds or flexible PVC liners. If you're considering such a purchase, try to get one with a more natural appearance, perhaps with an irregular shape. Nature generally doesn't create a perfectly round, or for that matter rectangular, pond, and you will find it much easier to integrate a non-uniform pond into your garden.

📷 THE BIRDWATCHER'S VEHICLE

Around once a month – or a little more infrequently if I'm honest – my car is transformed into the very model of organisational perfection. Sadly, this utopian state of affairs never lasts long.

Everything starts out well intentioned. The binoculars are in their case stowed on the Velcro spot on the dashboard. The maps are all folded and ready in their case. The pens and notebooks are all gathered in the console compartment. All seats are available for use. And the floor in the back is pristine.

One sighting later, all is chaos. The back seat a field table for planning the next manoeuvre. The maps disordered and crumpled. The binoculars vanished to some hard-to-reach part of the trunk. There are many positives to the on-the-go lifestyle of an active birder, but a tidy car is not one of them.

📷 BIRDING FROM THE WATER

I've been to spots on some lakes that had been visited by only a handful of humans in the previous 50 or 100 years. I've glided within near touching distance of bald eagles feeding on freshly snagged trout and cautiously wading herons without ruffling so much as a feather of alarm. Birding by water can put you in remote and isolated places, and give you a refreshingly different perspective on what you find there.

My particular preference is to use a canoe or kayak, because of the accessibility they offer on all sorts of water. However, craft of all sizes and descriptions can lead a birdwatcher to special opportunities – and I never pass up the chance to get out on the water.

Moreover, not only are you treated to a different perspective on the birds you seek, but you are also allowed the time to reflect. There is little in life that is more relaxing and more rewarding than birdwatching from the water.

Take to the water and leave the throngs of other birdwatchers behind as you move into new realms inhabited by new birds.

UNDERSTANDING HABITAT

A lot can be understood about birds by understanding their habitats. Each species has its own specialised demands, and seeks a habitat that can meet them. These can be crudely divided into four basic requirements: food; water; shelter from predators and the weather, and as a safe place to rear young; and adequate space.

In a completely natural world, the species and the elements of its habitat have evolved together over the millennia. Each species has become adapted, both physically and behaviourally, to take the best advantage of its habitat.

And, in many instances, elements of that habitat have co-evolved to take something they need from the animal as well. One instance of this are the trumpet-shaped flowers in the Americas, which employ nectar-feeding hummingbirds to carry pollen from one plant to the next.

A WIDER VIEW

On the broader stage, habitat loss is being blamed for the decline of thousands of species of birds worldwide. Even in the Western world – where the habitat is relatively stable in comparison to some areas in which rampant deforestation is ongoing – some species of birds have declined by as much as 90 percent since the 1960s. With a growing portion of the landscape occupied by humans and their demands, some scientists believe we're now at the point of deciding which populations we want to keep.

MAKING A DIFFERENCE

It may not have a substantial effect against that trend, but each of us with a piece of the suburban pie can do a bit to return some of our land to something other than that closely shaven, tightly manicured landscape so typical today. The birds will thank us for anything we can do. And, it certainly will be a much more interesting place in which to live.

From every living thing's perspective, habitat offers four key elements: food, water, shelter and adequate space.

📷 BIRD FEEDERS

As many fishing lures are designed primarily to catch fishermen, and the contents of their wallets, I firmly believe some bird feeders are designed more to attract the people who buy them than the birds that they feed. I honestly don't believe any bird really cares if its snack comes from a replica of a bright red barn or an acrylic cat's mouth. On the other hand, those novelty feeders can add a spark to the backyard, if that's the kind of thing you like. I'm more concerned with those feeder manufacturers who make overblown claims for the performance of their feeders.

Choosing the right feeder comes down to knowing which birds you want to attract and the manner in which they want to take their seed. The permutations of these two factors can be served by a few basic types of feeders – anything more is either decoration or gimmickry.

TUBE FEEDERS

Tube feeder are the most popular among the bird-feeding public today. Bin feeders were once preferred, back when more of us were building our feeders, primarily of wood, as it's much easier to build a box than a tube. However, now that we mostly use manufactured feeders, the seed-saving, easily hung and refilled tube feeders are king.

As the name implies, a tube feeder is a cylinder with a lid-covered opening at the top for filling, some form of hanging mechanism, and a series of small holes and perches along the sides for the birds to eat from. The feeding holes are available in a variety of sizes to accommodate different seed types.

A modern variation is the finch feeder, with the perches placed above the feeding holes, which are themselves tiny slits. The finch feeder is intended to offer the rather expensive niger seed to just a few species of highly prized finch that hang upside-down to feed, such as the American goldfinch, while excluding all other species from the feast.

Tube feeders are almost always hanging feeders. They are intended to be easily lifted and lowered for refilling and cleaning. However, recently, some very large tube-like feeders have hit the market, their size demanding some sort of support pole beneath their bases.

BIN FEEDERS

A bin feeder involves a container filled with a quantity of seed that is gradually released into feeding toughs or trays on opposite sides at the bottom of the bin. As the birds eat from a trough more seeds fall from above to take the place of those that have been consumed. However, bin feeders are rather wasteful of seed, as birds

Bin feeders offer large capacities for holding and dispensing significant quantities of seed over extended periods. They can be used in a variety of ways.

regularly develop the habit of pushing less preferred seeds out of the trough or tray to get to the food they like best. Bin feeders can be hung, but very often are mounted atop a pole.

PLATFORM FEEDERS

Platform feeders are much less popular than either the tube or bin feeder. They can be anything from a wide board placed on the ground, legs or a pole, to a flat boulder used for dispensing seeds. The idea is simple: a flat surface on which you spread seed for birds that prefer not to feed from a perched position. Doves, pigeons, blackbirds and sparrows are big on ground-feeding, which platforms basically replicate in a way that wastes a lot less seed.

SUET FEEDERS

Suet feeders are wire cages, mesh bags and the like into which bits of suet or suet cakes are deposited. Birds cling right to the cage or bag to pluck away at the suet inside. The mesh bags tend to wear out quickly under the constant assault of beaks and claws.

HUMMINGBIRD FEEDERS

For North American readers, a hummingbird feeder is yet another contraption that you can add to your garden. It consists of an enclosed reservoir to hold a supply of nectar to gradually feed into downward-facing tubes or upward-facing holes – very often decorated to look like flowers. Some include perches, but many do not. A larger variation is the oriole feeder, which is most often coloured orange.

Like many others caught up in backyard feeding, my feeding station includes several feeders of each of the above types – although the hummingbird and oriole feeders only come out during spring through to early autumn. At any given time, there might be eight to a dozen feeders in operation, not counting those for hummers and orioles. Needing a small wagon to transport the quantity of seeds my feeders run through every few days may be a bit extreme, but it does attract an array of species in considerable numbers throughout the year.

I write this as if feeding birds is some new and passing fad, and I'm its foremost proponent. But bird feeding is actually steeped in history. Even the Chinese Emperor Xuande had his artisans create the special blue-and-white porcelain bird feeders he personally filled during his reign in the fifteenth century. Now that's extreme!

ⓘ DOLING OUT NESTING MATERIALS

The spring I gave the cocker spaniel a haircut in the backyard – and did a rather poor job of cleaning up the mass of matted fur – was the year of blond birds' nests throughout the neighbourhood. Like shoppers at a clearance sale, the birds queued up to carry away huge quantities of the stuff to provide a comfortable lining for their nests.

The next spring we offered bits of natural yarn, cut to sizes that would not ensnare or harm the birds – and the result was the same.

The nesting materials you want to offer can be hung over tree or shrub limbs, tangled in brambles, jammed into tree crevices or stuffed loosely into a mesh bag that is then hung somewhere in the backyard like a tube feeder.

More natural nesting materials that arise through your normal garden work, such as lawn trimmings and pulled weeds, can be offered in the natural state by simply allowing them to lie where they fall. Most gardens tend to be a touch too neat and orderly for my tastes anyway.

Similarly, mud is used by many birds in building their nests – and it can be hard to come by in dry years – so consider dedicating a corner of your backyard to a muddy puddle. You can keep it in good supply by raking up the soil and giving it a regular dousing with the hose.

ARTIFICIAL MATERIALS

Care must be exercised in offering artificial materials to birds. For example, the plastic grass parents use to line their children's Easter baskets could be deadly to the birds using it and will remain in the environment for thousands of years. Likewise, the dyes in some coloured papers are toxic, so it is best to stick with

Many species of birds will eagerly accept a huge variety of materials, from garden clippings to human hair, and incorporate them all into the nests they are building.

shredded plain paper – although not the treated super-white kind.

Dryer lint would be readily taken by birds, but it tends to retain moisture for a very long time after even the briefest of rainfall, and therefore could draw precious heat away from eggs and nestlings.

In short, don't be afraid to offer the birds a helping hand, but before you do so consider whether your offerings will actually be a help or a hindrance – if in doubt, keep it natural.

◗◗ TOP BINOCULAR TECHNIQUE

There was a time when a dozen birders, including me, would suddenly spot the same bird a short distance into the undergrowth. A dozen pairs of binoculars would be lifted to a dozen pairs of eyes. A half-dozen birders would have the bird in view almost instantly. Another three or four would get their lenses on the bird within a minute or two. But, almost inevitably, among the last couple desperately panning around without a clue would be me.

That was until a kindly old-timer taught me how to use binoculars properly, beginning with the soft rubber eyecups at the back of the lens arrays, which were totally incompatible with my eyeglasses. Fold down the rubber and put the flat eyepiece against the lenses of your glasses, he told me. Ah, now that's so much better!

Now, he said, become familiar with the central focus for your binoculars, the wheel over the hinge between the two barrels of the optics that you turn back and forth to get a sharp, clear image.

Then he gave me the piece of the puzzle I was missing, the piece that very few guides on binoculars offer the reader: Adjust each eyepiece individually before going afield.

Select something like a sign that has clear, sharp lines as your test subject. Set the adjustable eyepiece on the right lens to the zero mark on its scale, close your right eye and adjust for the left eye using the central focus wheel. Then, with the left adjustment still in place, close your left eye and adjust for the right eye with the adjustable eyepiece. At that point, with both eyes now open, the sign should be in sharp focus. (Most binoculars have the adjustable eyepiece on the right, but if the pair in question has it on the left just switch the instructions.)

To double-check the adjustment, pick a second object at a different distance and, with both eyes open, turn the central focus ring to bring it into sharp focus. Alternately, close your left and then your right eyes. The image should remain in focus for both eyes. If it's not, you need to do a bit of additional adjustment, following the same process as before, but making changes in only very small increments.

Proper focal adjustment can be the difference between making a sighting and missing it.

👓 HELPING BABY BIRDS

Is there anything so helpless as a newly hatched chick? I'm talking about the chicks of altricial birds — robins, jays, cardinals, doves and for that matter most other birds — in other words, those that hatch all featherless and naked, with their eyes closed and totally dependent on their parents for everything.

It's the altricial babies that we most often encounter in our gardens, whether in a precariously balanced nest on a window ledge or when knocked from their home by a passing storm. Precocial chicks – such as geese and ducks – on the other hand, hatch with a full covering of soft down, their eyes open and their wits about them. They are ready to fend for themselves just a short while after breaking through the eggshell.

If you are faced with a stranded altricial chick then getting it back into the nest is the best course of action. It's an urban myth that the parent birds will reject them if they smell of humans. Just locate the nest and put the baby back with the minimum of fuss.

PLAN B

If, however, the nest has been destroyed, many species of garden birds will accept replacement nests. A small produce-counter basket, or a butter tub – with small holes punched in the bottom for drainage – can be wired into place where the nest formerly sat. If the original nest can be salvaged and placed inside the tub, then that's great. However, if the original is too badly damaged, form a new nest out of soft but dry grasses inside the replacement. Then return the baby or babies to the nest. The adult birds will probably show some scepticism about the new nest at first, but the demanding calls of their young will soon override that concern.

Your first action on finding baby birds should be to make absolutely certain that the babies are in fact abandoned.

REARING A CHICK

If there is absolutely no way to return the baby to its nest and you are certain that circumstances have led to its abandonment by the parents (and you really do need to be certain of that) then you may need to take steps to rescue the baby. However, be aware of the challenge you're taking on: baby birds must be fed every 15 minutes or so throughout the entire day, sunrise to sunset – so it's not something that a part-timer can really take on. The best course of action is to take a few simple steps, spelt out here, and then get a wildlife rehabilitator involved.

Obviously the chance of success for the average person is exceedingly low. But if there truly is no other choice and you just can't bring yourself to let nature take its course, place the baby inside a small, dark box with holes punched into the lid. Place a heating pad, set on low, beneath the box, or a 40-watt light bulb a little way above the box. Do not add grass inside the box, as that will do more harm than good. If you feel you must add 'nesting' material use paper towels. All through this process, handle the baby as little as possible and don't talk to the bird. Food will soon become the most urgent need for the baby, but initially the minimisation of all possible sources of stress is critical.

As soon as you have the baby settled in, call a professional. You've come to the end of what you can reasonably expect to accomplish yourself. Trying to feed it some homemade concoction such as bits of bread soaked in milk or honey, or even finding and feeding it bugs will probably kill the poor thing. Similarly, attempting to use an eyedropper will more than likely end in disaster.

PRECOCIAL CHICKS
Although they can gather most of their own food, even precocial chicks are vulnerable if separated from their parent. Again, the help they need is that of a professional.

The best remedy for precocial foundlings, or even altricial fledglings that are now feathered, is to herd them into a safe spot in your garden where the parents can find them. Maintain a quiet watch over them from a reasonable distance – a concealed or hidden spot is best – to make sure no cats take advantage of the situation, and wait for the parents to return. It usually will be just a matter of minutes after everything quiets. If they're still there after a few hours, then it's probably time to call a professional.

Safe Structures for Birds

One day there were three baby bluebirds nestled comfortably inside a nestbox near where I live. The next day there was one large blacksnake with three bulges in its belly. Unlike a metal post or a fence post with a surrounding baffle, the wooden post on which the nestbox was mounted presented the snake with easy access.

The good things we do for birds can also have downsides, such as a nestbox being too open to a predator's raid, or a feeder being too close to cover for bird-snatching cats. Even if we don't, nature always considers both sides of the coin and exploits what it finds. It's worth remembering that while we can dabble in the natural world, it's often hard to foresee all the outcomes of our actions. That shouldn't put you off lending nature a helping hand, but neither should you be surprised when things don't turn out as you planned.

Whatever you do to help out the birds, you can never be quite sure of the outcome.

MAKING BIRD TREATS

Many of us like to find an additional connection with our garden birds by cooking for them, and suet pine cones are a tried-and-tested treat that are always much appreciated.

Several pine cones will be needed and they should be gathered as a first step in your garden or a nearby park. Cones with scales that have opened fully are better.

3. Place the suet in a pan and slowly melt it down over low heat.

1. Twist one end of a long piece of wire to the point of each pine cone.

4. When the suet has liquefied from the first heating, allow it to cool back to a solid and then melt it a second time. This is a process known as 'double rendering'.

2. You'll also need a few large chunks of beef suet, which is generally available from the meat counter in the supermarket, and usually for reasonable prices.

5. After the second melting, allow the liquid suet to cool again. After five minutes or so, stir in a handful of two of the seed mix you use in your feeders.

6. Allow the mix to cool for a few more minutes, then slowly roll and dip your pine cones into it, coating as much of each cone's surface with the mixture as possible.

7. Stand the cones on a sheet of waxed paper on a plate and place in the refrigerator for several hours.

8. After the suet-seed mix has hardened, hang your new bird feeders by the loose ends of the wires from tree branches in your backyard.

ALTERNATIVE TREATS

The same suet mix can be poured into cookie or muffin moulds and allowed to harden into homemade suet cakes, which then can be used exactly like the cakes bought in the shops. Another use for the mix, just before it hardens completely – when it's the consistency of cake frosting with sprinkles in it – is to spread it on trees, posts, rocks and the like in the garden, thereby converting any useful surface into an additional feeder.

A useful source of additional seed for backyard feeding is the nearest patch of weeds or wildflower meadow. With the permission of the owner, gather bunches of old, dry weed stems that still have their spent flower or seed heads attached. The best are those that still offer the most nutrition, with the most seeds still attached.

Form a swag by bundling handfuls of the seed-laden stems together with a wire around their bases. Use another wire to hang each swag from feeder post, fence post, trees or wherever you like, where the birds will cling to them while taking the seeds.

In the spirit of an Easter egg hunt, scatter a bagful of in-the-shell peanuts around your backyard, placing a few peanuts in every nook and cranny, from the trunks of trees to the crooks where branches join the trunks, from the tops of fence posts to ground-covering vines.

Whole peanuts are particular favourites for many bird species. Not to mention squirrels, which will spend many entertaining hours searching until they've found the last of them.

BINOCULARS BY THE NUMBERS

Binoculars are a fairly basic bit of technology, but one that happens to be central to the pursuit of birdwatching. Understanding and using that technology to its maximum can help give you that extra edge when you're out in the field.

The core numbers for every pair of binoculars are expressed as an equation such as 8x32. The number on the left is the magnification provided by the binoculars – in our example, that would be eight times normal eyesight. The second number, on the right, is the diameter of the lens at the front of the binoculars, also known as the objective. The larger that number, the more light is allowed to enter the binoculars and the better the image through the binoculars will be, especially under low-light conditions. For example, a 50 mm objective lets in about twice the light of a 35 mm objective. Of course, as both sides of the equation grow larger, the binoculars grow heavier and more difficult to hold steady. What's more, the price tag grows as well. For example, a 10x70 pair can weigh as much as twice a 7x50 pair and move right out of the price bracket of many casual birders.

OTHER CONSIDERATIONS

Another critical number is the field of view, which is a measure of the width of a scene in view 1,000 yards or so in front of the binoculars. A wider field of view will make finding birds through the binoculars easier, but the pay-off is being less able to resolve details in the scene.

Similarly, the larger the exit pupil, which is the size of the image at the focusing point of the binoculars, the easier it will be to keep your eye on the image in bright light and the brighter will be the image. The size of the exit pupil is calculated by dividing the diameter of the front lens by the magnification power.

Eyeglass wearers with astigmatisms – meaning they need to wear their glasses while using binoculars – will be particularly interested in the eye relief number of the binoculars.

Binoculars are the key birdwatching tool, and understanding all those numbers will help you get the pair that suit you best.

Eye relief is the distance behind the ocular, or rear, lens of the binoculars at which the image is in focus. Too long an eye relief will project the image behind the corrective lens of the eyeglasses. For most eyeglass wearers, an eye relief of 15 mm will be about right.

Infinity is an easy focus point for nearly all binoculars. Close-up is not so easy to achieve. Basic, cheap binoculars generally will focus on objectives no closer than 20 ft (6 m) or so. A much better choice for birdwatching is a close focus of 10 ft (3 m) or less.

The number of coatings on the lenses of a binoculars is another key numerical consideration. Lenses are coated to reduce the amount of light lost to reflection off the lens surface and increase the light transmitted through the glass. Without any coating the reflective loss per lens can be as much as 5 percent, but can be reduced to just a few tenths of a percent per lens with multiple coatings.

Then you have the physical attributes of the binoculars, but these can't be distilled to simple numbers. When it comes to how they feel in the hand, there's only one way to find out – and that's to get down to the shops and try a few pairs.

🔭 SPOTTING SCOPES

Why is it that amateur astronomers with long-lensed optics mounted atop tripods seem to always be such nice, sharing people, ready to let others sneak a peek through the telescope; but birdwatchers with spotting scopes on tripods seem to be territorial birding snobs that would prefer you just keep moving rather than catch a glimpse of 'their bird'?

Aside from the size of their optics, which can be fairly similar, what is it that makes the two groups react so differently to other people? Could it be something about all astronomers generally needing longer lenses, but the birding scopes somehow representing a step up to some higher level of birding? The scopes certainly do raise the minimum investment for even entry level optics – and perhaps those that use them look down on those who don't. Or is it perhaps my own bias – a form of scope envy, so to speak?

Do spotting scopes represent a true advance in optical capability or just a snobbish symbol?

BRUSH PILES FOR BIRDS

Brush piles attract birds, particularly many of our garden species. However, brush piles can also anger our neighbours, not least those who take pride in their carefully manicured lawns and regimented flower beds.

Brush piles are a naturally occurring feature of many ecosystems, particularly in the temperate regions in which so many of us live. Building a brush pile or two on a site that was carved from the natural landscape to make way for a home is, in a way, giving something back to nature.

Because they are a feature that birds have come to relate to over hundreds of generations, brush piles are a magnet to many of the species we want to attract into our gardens. They offer shelter from the elements, protection and an escape route from enemies, and sometimes food in the form of the insects that often inhabit them and the plants that grow over them.

Some of the more common species may begin using brush piles within a few hours of their construction. More unusual species may take longer, but they will make use of them when they come across them.

So what's the downside? Well, brush piles can fall foul of local regulations, so it's best to do a little research. At this stage you're probably not seeking a permit, just acquainting yourself with the local bylaws to avoid conflict.

One common complaint is that brush piles attract vermin, but only easily and

Garden brush piles do not attract vermin unless there also are nearby sources of food, which is the real attraction for rats and mice.

regularly available sources of food do that. Okay, a mouse or two might take advantage of spilled seed, but it's not enough to attract rodents that aren't already nearby.

As with everything, there are pros and cons; however, from the birdwatching point of view, the positives far outweigh the negatives.

BUILDING A BRUSH PILE

Building a brush pile is simple. Stack all your woody yard trimmings loosely in a mound, leaving small openings among the materials and regular openings to the outside world. Place your softer waste, such as vines and weeds, over the top of the woody material, keeping that loose and taking care not to block any of the openings. Add additional material as it becomes available in the course of tending your garden.

The brush pile's placement is a key consideration, especially with respect to your neighbours. An out-of-the-way corner at the back of the property is ideal, especially if it is next to a hedge.

Even then it may be best to keep your neighbours sweet by concealing the pile, which can be accomplished in a number of easy ways. Privacy-type fencing might be erected around the brush pile, or shrubs might be planted around it. Vining plants, including ornamentals such as wisteria, can even be planted around the edges of the pile and trained to grow up and over it.

A BETTER PILE

Any pile of limbs and other trimmings will attract and benefit birds, but there is a recipe for an even more effective and beneficial design. In a basic brush pile, the materials will gradually settle, closing off many of the interior openings as well as entrances and exits. However, you can shore up those openings, and even create larger and more beneficial ones inside the brush pile, by adding a grid of timbers, similar to the way in which a door has a frame.

Begin the brush pile by laying a grid frame right on the ground, topped by a second grid. Then pile wood on top of and within the grid. When it has reached thigh height add another timber grid right on top of the garden trimmings. Continue the brush pile on top of that new gridwork, adding a new grid at regular intervals.

If you have lots of outdoor space and no worries about annoying your neighbours, consider building a number of brush piles in a number of places. Next to the flower or vegetable garden will bring in insect-eating birds; in full view of a window obviously offers easy birdwatching opportunities; while wildlife experts would recommend placing one close to a forested area, or near waterways or wetlands, to enhance the benefits to wildlife.

GETTING STARTED

On a final note, if you want to get birds moving into your new brush pile quickly, then toss a few handfuls of seed around and over the pile. You might even consider hanging a feeder over it, but make sure it is well out of reach of any would-be predators such as the neighbourhood cat.

THE COMFORT FACTOR

Younger readers may not appreciate this, but after a certain age each passing year brings with it a few more aches and pains, and a greater appreciation for every little additional comfort, even on the birdwatching trail. Just because we need to maintain a good degree of mobility doesn't mean we can't arrive and enjoy the birds in comfort. Brand names aside, my ever-increasing list of comforting extras is as follows.

A lightweight, collapsible camp stool is a much nicer perch than a hard boulder or tick-infested log. However, a recent twist has taken this basic bit of gear to the next level – a swivelling seat that allows me to turn for a quick look in any given direction without needing to jump up and reposition the entire stool.

CLOTHING
Lightweight, breathable shell jackets, which seem to get lighter each year, combined with layers of high-tech insulation inside have pretty much defeated cold, wet weather conditions. Add a few dry chemical hot packs and I'm downright toasty all day long. Recently I found an ultra-lightweight, waterproof, sweat-wicking pair of mitten-gloves, with mitten slots that open to allow the free use of the synthetically housed fingers.

Several years ago it looked as if boot developers had reduced the weight and enhanced the waterproof and wicking abilities about as much as they could. But they never stopped their R&D and footwear comfort has been advancing nearly every year.

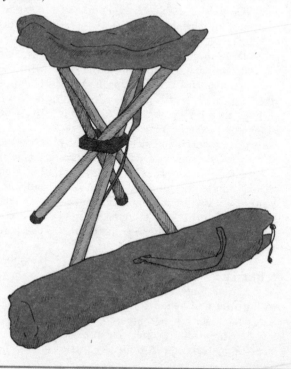

My extended birdwatching outings have been made immeasurably more enjoyable by the addition of a comfortable camp stool.

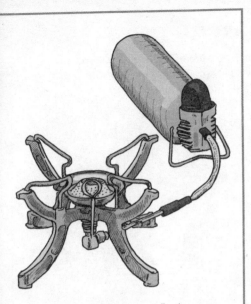

A hot meal in the field can really cheer you up, especially when the weather is miserable and there's not a bird in sight.

COOKING KIT

Palm-sized backpacking stoves with fuel canisters nearly as small, and a lightweight stove-top-ready cup, have made having a hot drink in the field into a comfort booster with practically no downside. Even water bottles are growing ever lighter, although water itself resolutely weighs just the same as it ever did.

In many aspects of my life I'm all for a return to simpler, more natural materials and methods. However, I readily admit that, when it comes to my comfort in the field, the march of high-technology has been very good to me.

A birdwatching couple I know hosts an elaborate party every spring for their friends. The day begins with some good-natured birding competition along prearranged and randomly drawn routes, with a prize for the winning team. It ends in a late afternoon feast, planned, cooked and served along some fascinating theme.

To date, their most memorable dinner has been styled after the traditional Victorian English picnic. They reasoned that Victorian Englishmen and women were among the first to pursue birdwatching as a hobby and probably ate a few picnics while they were trekking after the birds.

Apparently those Victorians could really put it away. The menu for our feast included cold roast beef, cold boiled beef, cold lamb, cold pheasant, cold duck, ham, pickled beef tongue, warm veal and ham, vegetable pies, cold lobster, spring salad with cucumbers, stewed dried fruits with tea biscuits, cheesecake with berries, fruited bread pudding with cream, almond-flavoured flan, and cream puff pastries filled with jam. It was all washed down with black English gunpowder tea, served hot or cold, with lemon or cream.

We ate on cloth tablecloths spread on the lawn; and it certainly beat the squashed sandwiches that I usually pull from the bottom of my pack.

COOKING WHILE WATCHING

My late mother never made a birding trip outside of her own garden, but she was avid about the activity in her own way. A large wooden bin feeder my father made for her was the centre of her birding world.

It stood on a pole outside the kitchen window, which was the room where mother spent most of her time, keeping the family in homemade meals and snacks. She was particularly enamoured of the evening grosbeaks that regularly irrupted south from Canada in the winter.

In one of the oldest memories I have of her, she is leaning on a table at that kitchen window with a wooden cooking spoon in one hand and an Audubon field guide to the birds of eastern North America in the other. I think that field guide was one of the first gifts I ever saved up my allowance and bought for her.

I wonder how many of today's birders have similar memories of their parents at the kitchen window watching the backyard birds and how many of tomorrow's birders will have memories of us in the same situation. The kitchen window really is one of the best birdwatching spots you could hope for.

There's little better than cooking and watching birds at the same time, so here's a recipe to keep you busy and them fed. Render a half-pound of suet. In a separate bowl, mix together a half-cup of black oil sunflower seeds, a half-cup of millet, a quarter-cup of chopped peanuts and a quarter-cup of chopped raisins. Stir the rendered suet into the mixture. Pour the mixture into moulds then refrigerate until it hardens.

🔭 DRESSING THE PART

Birdwatchers have been the focus of a stereotyped image for a very long time. The most recent incarnation is best typified by the 1960s American sitcom, The Beverly Hillbillies. Played by actress Nancy Kulp, the character Miss Jane Hathaway, secretary to the conniving banker Milburn Drysdale, was the overly serious, super-enthusiastic birdwatcher. When she went in pursuit of this or that species, she donned something that looked very much like a Boy Scout uniform, above-the-knee socks and all. It's an image that haunts birdwatchers from all corners of the globe still.

We don't see that garb all that much today, at least not among birders. As a leader in the Boy Scouts, I confess we do wear such uniforms at ceremonies and the like. Birders, however, can normally no longer be identified by what they're wearing – perhaps just by an eagerly clutched field guide or pair of binoculars.

While you may no longer be able to tell a birder apart by dress, the attitude of some of our number still sets them apart from the crowd. There's the brow furrowed in concentration and the firmly set jaw in the face of adverse weather. Yes, even though there's no set uniform it's sometimes possible to spot a birder by that a look of concentration that still accompanies a quest of unimaginable import.

An overly serious and zealous attitude about birdwatching can lead to what non-birders might see as eccentric behavior, and for that matter even eccentric dress.

🔭 SAMPLING YOUR GARDEN BIRDS

Birds are famously reluctant to answer interviewers' questions. As a matter of fact, short of a few trained parrots, it is downright impossible to even get a 'no comment' out of the entire avian community. And yet we know a great deal about what they like to eat, just because researchers have spent the time watching them. Even if you lack a white lab coat, you can perform the same experiments in your own backyard.

Start with several types of seed, nothing in a mix, just a couple of handfuls each of the individual seed types. A good cross-section includes black oil sunflower, striped sunflower, safflower, red millet, white millet, milo, peanut hearts, rice and hulled wheat.

Arrange old plates or flat rocks, all of about the same dimensions, a little way apart somewhere in your garden. You can be really scientific about this by eliminating all extra variables; for example, try to put all the plates or rocks in a similar setting and so on.

Onto the plates or rocks spread an equal amount of each of the seeds you've chosen for the experiment, just one type to each plate or rock. Note which seed type is on each and retire to a hidden spot somewhere nearby or inside where a window looks out onto your test area. You might want to have a notebook and pen or pencil handy. Also, glance at the clock and note the time.

WAIT AND SEE

Make yourself comfortable with a cosy chair and nice beverage, and wait. When the first birds arrive at your seed array, note the time that has elapsed, the species of bird, the number of

each species and the seed they decide to eat. Repeat this process for the next birds to show up and so on. If a bird first

Given the opportunity, in a structured way, garden birds will tell the attentive birdwatcher everything about their feeding preferences.

arrives at one type of seed but changes its mind and moves to another, note that as well.

When one type of seed is exhausted, make a note of that along with the elapsed time. Don't replace it just yet: instead watch carefully to see if the birds then move to a second stash.

Make notes of everything you observe for a few hours and you'll begin to see how the birds are telling you the types of seed they would rather you bought for them. The optimum times to conduct this experiment are early morning or late afternoon, when birds will be most active in their search for food.

SOMETHING A LITTLE DIFFERENT

A variation of this experiment – which actually more closely replicates the method used by the landmark seed-preference studies that bird writers now all refer to – would be to elevate the feeding stations into a long, partitioned feeder tray. It could also be accomplished by offering the different seed types each in their own bin-type feeders. Tube feeders could be used; however, they limit the variety of birds that will take advantage of the opportunity, and thus introduce another variable to the experiment.

However you decide to conduct your own version of this experiment, I promise you will amaze yourself with the insight you gain into the birds in your garden.

FEEDING BEYOND WINTER

The perception of birds as being dependent upon our garden feeders is flawed. While winter feeding doubtless lends a helping hand, the whole reason that we feed birds is because of the pleasure they give us, so there's no real need to stop during the summer months.

Leaving the feeders up and refilled all year round is neither hurting nor much helping the birds, which have plenty of other food sources available to them. Making sure that they are still attracted to your feeders, however, can be more of a challenge as there is a greater abundance of food for them to choose from.

In order to mitigate this it's important that you know the feeding habits of the birds that frequent your garden (see p. 28 and left). It's also important to be a little more disciplined with your feeding, as it is that much easier for feed to spoil in the warmer weather.

Summer feeding does have plenty of advantages, however, as it will often bring birds into your garden that you wouldn't see during the winter. Furthermore, it gives you the chance to see some birds all year round, and to witness how their appearance and behaviour changes throughout the seasons.

CREATING BIRD HABITAT

Assuming you want to make a difference to the bird life in your back garden — and people increasingly do — one way of making a change is to improve what your garden offers in the way of a suitable habitat. This doesn't mean it has to be unattractive, quite the contrary — the influx of birds will reward you with a more vibrant backyard, one that is humming with life.

It all comes down to determining the needs of the species that you want to lure to your backyard. First you should consider what is already in place that can help towards that end. Then think about adding more natural and native elements to meet the birds' needs. And finally consider supplemental features that can be incorporated to give everything a bit of a boost.

Every species of bird has habitat preferences that will attract it to a specific location.

FOOD AND WATER

Many backyard birds are primarily insect eaters, but they are also willing to take in a fair amount of seeds, fruits and nuts. The easiest way to increase a variety of food types is by introducing native plants under a plan that mixes plants according to the time of year they are producing, to achieve a supply of food well spaced across the calendar. Bird feeders, although not a natural source, can also be incorporated.

Water is discussed in greater detail elsewhere (see p. 60), but from the perspective of the overall habitat a water feature of some sort will act as a real magnet and make your garden a far more attractive proposition to many species of bird.

SPACE AND SHELTER

When the mating and nesting season arrives other demands will come to the fore. At that time of the year, suitable places to nest and raise young will be a huge attraction to prospective tenants, especially if they're well integrated into your backyard landscape. However, different species have different demands, so it pays to become familiar with those that typically nest in your area, learning their shelter needs and providing for them accordingly.

As is the case with bird feeders serving as a supplement to natural sources of food, nestboxes are a fine supplement to the natural availability of hollow trees for the bird species we know as 'cavity nesters'. Again, it pays to be aware of what local species prefer, as the array of nestboxes available is quite large.

Further to a place to nest, native trees, shrubs and herbaceous plants will also offer shelter from both predators and the elements, and it is worth considering creating your own brush pile.

🔭 BIRD BATHS

Bird baths are a good way of inviting more species into your garden. And there are good reasons they have been so popular for so long, as they are a quick, easy, relatively cheap and low-maintenance form of attraction for a variety of birds.

Provided that they are no deeper than two inches (50 mm) at their deepest nor too slippery for birds to hold their footing, birds will generally feel safe while dipping in a bird bath. A waist-high pedestal raises the bath enough to give the birds a jump start over approaching ground-based predators, such as the neighbour's cat. While placing the bath a little way from shrubs and trees with low-hanging branches will offer quick escape routes from all threats.

When positioning, or repositioning, a birdbath, remember that a bathing bird is at a disadvantage with its wet feathers. Its take-off will be a bit slower than normal. Its flight won't be as quick and sure as when it's dry. Birds are well aware of this and so a location that offers a degree of security will help ensure your bath is well used.

On the flipside, however, it's worth noting that you can take the idea too far. Don't place the birdbath close to any branches or shrubs where a predator might lurk in wait for a quick pounce.

OTHER VISITORS

Bird baths also attract some insect life. Some of these are beautiful in their own right, and even those that aren't will often attract more birds. What's more, don't be surprised if someone else takes advantage of your largesse – it's not uncommon to see a squirrel leap up onto the rim to grab a quick drink.

Most backyard birds prefer baths that are not too deep and also offer a little traction underfoot.

UNDERSTANDING BIRD SEED

A quick quiz: side by side in a store you find the following: A sack of mixed bird seed that is about one-quarter rice, hulled oats, milo and peanut hearts that few desired backyard bird species will eat. And, for the same price, a sack half the size of the first containing only black oil sunflower seeds. Which is the better value?

Although you may start out with more useful seed, even after the quarter of waste product is calculated out, the birds will eventually waste far more of the mixed seed as they try to sort through the chaff to get to what they want. There will be much less waste in the second, as the birds will take care to get to every kernel of goodness.

All bird seed is not created equal. Few of the bird species you want at your feeders will come for rice, hulled oats, milo or peanut hearts, which is the filler that packs many commercial seed mixes. That is not to say that all seed mixes are poorly formulated and a waste of your money. There are some very good mixes that serve a wide variety of bird species very well. A bit of label reading is all that's required to make an informed choice.

On the other hand, anyone who offers black oil sunflower, safflower, millet and

Many seed mixes available through grocers and other non-birding suppliers contain unacceptable levels of waste matter and seed types that most bird species simply do not prefer.

niger seed, each in its own feeder, will satisfy nearly all possible preferences among the garden birds in nearly any neighbourhood. Add a suet feeder to the array and everyone out there is satisfied.

Serving up those no-waste seeds will also be easier on your lawn and garden, with far less weedy growth from seeds the birds discard.

Choosing Seed

Black oil sunflower seed is the preferred seed among so many species because it delivers a relatively high-energy, high-protein kernel inside a thin, easily opened shell. Striped sunflower will also serve for many species, but even those will show preference for the black oil seeds. Safflower is a speciality seed particularly favoured by cardinals in North America, and is also off-putting to squirrels. Millet will satisfy the ground-foraging preferences for a number of sparrow and dove species. And the tiny, expensive niger seed is tailor-made to be offered in specially restrictive feeders just for a few sought-after species of finches. Suet is enjoyed by a great many species, but will be a special draw for woodpeckers and nuthatches.

Supplementing Seed

An additional food that some backyard feeders like to offer is corn. As cracked corn it is especially appealing to the ground-feeders. And, as either whole kernels or still on the cob, corn is a particularly good idea in those backyards along waterways, forests and other wild areas, as it will attract waterfowl, turkeys, pheasants and the like.

A food supplement that can really set one garden feeding station apart from all the others in the neighbourhood is grit.

Birds, having no teeth, don't chew, but instead a muscular, sack-like organ known as the gizzard performs that function. It is stocked with small hard things like sand and grit to help break the food down. You can offer a plate of such material right alongside your other feeder fillers – it is even available packaged at pet shops. In addition, baked and crumbled eggshells, and ground oyster shells, will be snatched up eagerly.

How Much is Enough?

I tend to offer as much seed and accessory items – all of the finest quality, of course – whenever I can. That way I don't feel as much guilt and frustration when things inevitably slip a bit. Most of us start with the best of intentions, buying the best seed and topping up our feeders on a daily basis. Then, some daily distraction pulls us away from our routine and the bird feeders take a back seat. That's not a major disaster – the birds often have plenty of other sources for their food.

However, you should be careful to store your seed well, as it can go stale if not stored properly in sealed containers. The next time you come to put it in your feeders you will most likely find that the birds ignore it. Also, if not stored properly, it can get damp and rot or sprout, which also renders it worse than useless.

Finally, when you are storing your seed, you should be careful to keep it well out of reach of any foraging rodents, as they will quickly track down and chew their way into containers packed with rich stores of seed.

▲▲ REMOTE PHOTOGRAPHY

With today's advancing technology it's now possible for even an amateur to get photos of birds without ever clicking a shutter themselves.

There are a number of advantages to remote photography, as it allows you to take shots you would be hard pushed to otherwise, and it can also help minimise the disturbance to the birds and other wildlife. This means it's an excellent way to monitor a nestbox or bird feeder and get some wonderfully candid images. After the camera has been in place for a few days, the birds will soon accept it as part of the landscape.

A number of specialised products exist, which can easily do the job. However, while some boast useful features such as camouflage and weatherproofing, the quality will normally be somewhat lower than that of a good digital camera. Therefore, one alternative worth thinking about, is combining a digital SLR, if you have one, with a remote motion sensor trigger. Sure, you'll still end up with the odd badly framed shot, but the quality of the file it produces will generally be higher.

What's more, the digital era has made sharing and printing images so much easier. And you needn't stick to still photography, as all-in-one nestbox and video camera packages are now available.

Whichever system you choose, the great thing is that viewing the shots on computer is packed full of surprises – you never know what you'll get.

▲▲ BLINDS

Telephoto lenses are great for tack-sharp close-ups. Spotting scopes draw in the pageantry from incredible distances. But only in a blind have I been so close to the birds that a wild turkey actually plucked a grasshopper from in front of my nose and the smack of a Cooper's hawk snatching a fleeing nuthatch was so close as to be almost tangible.

Blinds are key to close encounters with birdlife. They are also undergoing constant development with new high-tech materials, largely because of their popularity in the world of hunters. However, they can also be quite basic – as simple as a few walls of tree branches woven loosely or an old white sheet tossed over oneself while lying in a snow-covered meadow; or as complex as a small tent, with a number of poles and cords.

Buying Tip

As new high-tech materials are incorporated into the manufacture of blinds, their weight is falling fast and you now might be able to carry a larger blind than you would have wanted to just a year or two ago. Maybe a blind that accommodates two rather than one is now worth considering. Even if you use it on your own, it will be much more comfortable.

While the blind scraped together in-situ from whatever nature has left strewn about is convenient and requires no heavy lifting or transport, the commercially made blind being much like a tent has some of the same admirable qualities of comfort! It will keep the occupants relatively dry regardless of the weather outside, and just as importantly it will keep you relatively warm.

On the other hand, I've never had to chase down a field-made blind as it blew into a farmer's pond because I neglected to anchor it with stakes or cords tied to the brush. I've also never had a field-made blind stolen while it was being left in place to familiarise the birds with its presence.

Blinds allow for up-close observation of birds without having to rely on binoculars, a scope or a telephoto lens.

◉◉ BUILDING A HIDE

There's no point attracting the most amazing range of birds to your garden if you can't watch them without frightening them away. Depending on how much time you'll spend hidden away with your binoculars, hides can be anything from glorified evergreen 'igloos' with a viewing slot, to small huts with a comfortable old armchair.

WILLOW HIDES

A hide could just be a concrete box, but who wants that? You can make a terrific one out of lengths of woven growing willow, threaded through taught horizontal wires attached to wooden posts. Set them out in a square, leaving room for an entrance. You can buy the willow online, which usually comes in 6-ft (2-m) lengths. *Salix viminalis* is your best bet, and grows up to 12 ft (4 m) a year.

Dig a 6-in (15-cm) -wide trench in the ground and get planting. Firmly wedge the willow rods in the ground, 8–12 in (20–30 cm) deep and 12 in (30 cm) apart. Aim for a crisscross lattice, weaving them up, over, and under. Loosely tie the rods to keep them in place, and then train them to grow across the roof. Nip off the growing points when they're too

long. When the hide eventually becomes chock-a-block with new growth, and a massive thickening of stems, cut it back in winter and new shoots will quickly sprout out to give more cover.

HEDGE HIDES

Alternatively, you can grow a hedge hide using species like box or yew. You'll need a basic structure using pillars and posts linked by lengths of taught wire. Line up the box (which is brighter green than yew) about 12 in (30 cm) apart, and give a regular spring feed of seaweed fertiliser, which will generate strong plants that shouldn't be prone to disease. Keep giving a light all-over trim to force out lots of new, bushy side growth. You can cut out viewing holes, but if it's not in the right place, so what? The box will quickly grow over and fill the opening, and you can cut a different one.

The roof can be as ornate or as wild as you like. Best of all, create a green or turf roof by planting it with sedums, wildflowers, grasses and perennials. First, check that the structure can take

A step-by-step guide to building a willow hide. Growth on the stems will eventually thicken, and the lattice weaving will ensure a good, even coverage to hide you away.

Fig.1.	**Fig.2.**	**Fig.3.**	**Fig.4.**

a saturated green roof, and that it'll be waterproof (use a waterproof liner over the existing roof). Then fix in place a framework of boards with compartments giving a growing depth of 2–8 in (5–20 cm). Secure it in place, and then fill each compartment with a lightweight substrate such as crushed brick with some compost. Finally, plant up with drought-tolerant plants – and that's essential, unless you want to spend all summer watering your roof. This gives an incredibly natural-looking hide that'll also attract plenty of birds.

Location, Location

It's so obvious it sounds mad to say it, but your hide needs to give you a great view of the best mix of birds possible. If you're creating a brand-new bird garden, make sure that the various different habitats – pond, feeders, berrying shrubs, and a clear stretch of ground where birds can tap the ground to bring up worms – are in sight of the hide.

Fig.5.

Fig.6.

🔭 BIRDING ONLINE

Thousands of websites, chatrooms and the like all over the Internet want to be your go-to spot for all things birdwatching. I'm not going to list them here – the Internet is too changeable an environment – but here are a few pointers.

No matter what traditionalists might say, the web is a great place for birders. Yes, I like most people would rather be out in the field with my binoculars in hand, than sat in front of a screen. But there is more than enough room in most birders' lives for both.

The Internet frees you to travel anywhere you like – albeit virtually – regardless of whether you can afford the air fare. Now you can speak to birders all over the world, keep in touch with others' birding exploits and tell them about your own, no matter where they live.

A personal website is an ever more popular method of telling people about your birdwatching, particularly if you like to take photographs as well. And these are growing ever easier and cheaper to design and maintain.

Of course, the Internet's greatest blessing is the sheer quantity of information it offers. Without doubt the quality varies hugely, from a learned academic paper on migration, to the opinion and speculation of a bulletin board. But it doesn't take long to sort the wheat from the chaff, and it all adds to the pleasure of a life spent watching birds.

👀 WATCHING BIRDS WITH YOUR EARS

When undisturbed, birds are far from a silent lot. If you're not pressuring them, they are eager to announce themselves, their exact identity and their location. Birdsong and bird calls are an important component of bird identification, to both the birds and the humans who note their presence and observe them.

'Woodcock. Over there', whispered our bird club outing leader. Confusion spread across many faces in the gathering darkness. 'That "peent"… that was him', explained our leader. Some nodded in agreement, but plenty of others were far from certain just what it was.

Bird identification by song and call is a remarkable skill for those who are able to develop it. For those of us with tonal abilities of the kind that has our neighbours in the church pew edging away during hymns, it may be a slightly more distant goal. However, whatever your natural ear for a tune, like many other birding skills, the best place to develop it is in the field.

GETTING STARTED

Having the ability to identify different recorded songs is akin to being able to perform trigonometry on a well-developed problem in a textbook – neither matters a great deal until you put it to the test, in the field.

Developing the ability to pick up on the sounds of birds and to identify them using that evidence alone requires an adjustment to most people's mindset. We have evolved into an existence based largely on the sense of sight. Our world is in large part defined and made sense of to us through what we see. And the other senses often take second place to the dominance of sight.

Many other animals make far greater use of a range of senses to an extent that we could never emulate, but it is still possible to improve your skills. There is a kernel of truth in the folk-wisdom about a person's senses of hearing and smell improving in the wake of the loss of eyesight – not that the sense itself grows stronger, but that the individual learns to become better attuned to a particular sensory input. On a more trivial scale, if you sit and close your eyes for 15 or 20 minutes the next time you're in an outdoor setting, you'll most likely find it that much easier to concentrate on the songs and calls of the birds.

Aside from learning to focus on audible rather than visual signals, being able to identify a bird by its song also depends upon being able to pair a song with a bird. For this purpose there are plenty of field guides available. Just as a well-illustrated field guide is central to identification by sight, the best song field guides are those that are accompanied by a recording of the birdsong in question.

Such field guides will provide the generally accepted description of a bird's song using human words, such as the 'who cooks for you, who cooks for you-all' of the barred owl. Such anthropomorphisations of songs and calls have become generally accepted because many agree with their replication of the sounds of the bird. They are also useful because they are easy to remember and apply in the field, and they provide an easy way of communicating exactly what you mean to another birder. However, such mnemonics don't work for everyone – you might find that a different line does the trick. The critical thing is the association of a bird's song with something catchy, which will lock that song into your memory bank for good.

IN THE FIELD
Practising the application of the songs and calls you've learned is key to fixing them in your memory. Like a foreign language, it's all to easy to forget what you don't use regularly.

The early morning, especially in spring, is among the very best times for hearing the greatest variety of song and call for the longest duration. And this gives you a great chance to practise on a wide variety of species.

Nearly every bird species has a distinctive call, and that of the European song thrush is one of the most beautiful.

The wonderful aspect of being able to make a wide array of identifications by sound alone is the fact that the trained ear can pick up on many more birds than will ever present themselves within your line of sight.

This ability also opens up otherwise unexplored avenues, particularly in the case of birdwatching at night when it is all but impossible to make a sighting – it's truly amazing just how many birds sing after sunset. Or for that matter, you can enjoy a lazy Sunday morning lying in bed, listening to and identifying the birds in your own back garden.

IN DEFENCE OF BIRDWATCHING

Like any activity that makes use of the great outdoors, birdwatching has its detractors. But while some criticism is justified, birders in general are a powerful force for positive change.

Birders have long been portrayed in some quarters as overly focused, holier-than-thou elitists, placing their love of birds and birding above all else. The popular media have often poked fun at this stereotype of a binocular-clutching obsessive, taking it to its illogical extremes.

Meanwhile, groups with conflicting interests – hunters, for example – sometimes see birders as restriction-imposing, self-interested interlopers, and to be fair this is not always without some justification. Likewise, those whose livelihoods and economic interests can be at odds with the welfare of birds, such as farmers or the fishing community, often come into conflict with birders. Meanwhile, the government officials who must arbitrate between these groups' demands can find birders to be uncompromising to the exclusion of all other concerns.

Like all stereotypes, each of those depictions of birders is undoubtedly an exaggeration, but one that has a kernel of truth at its heart. Like many others, I've had the fun sucked out of birding expeditions in the past by companions who were too zealous for my tastes. But that is certainly the exception rather than the rule.

THE ENVIRONMENTAL IMPACT
Of course, by the very nature of our pursuit, many birders have an ingrained concern for the environment. And there are plenty of good causes I've seen birding groups working towards. However, it is sometimes the case that birders can be condescending to other groups.

The chief distinction between outdoor activities is whether they are low-impact or high-impact – categories that are usually based on whether something dies in the process. For example, birders, hikers and catch-and-release fishermen are often classed as low-impact users, while hunters and trappers are considered to be high-impact users. However, given the high-tech, travel-intensive birding that is practised by many today, the high–low distinction is no longer so clear. Can a birder who flies halfway around the world to see a particular species really be considered to have a low impact?

The kiwis of New Zealand represent the best and worst of human intervention, as conservation groups fight hard to save them from extinction.

Furthermore, it is worth considering the relationship between your hobby and your wider lifestyle. It's all too easy to be concerned about nature when you're immersed in the great outdoors, only to forget about it once you're ensconced in your home again.

That being said, taken as a whole birders are among the most effective, dedicated and generous of the outdoor groups, and are working at all levels to save birds and their habitats. They are making immense contributions of money, effort and time. And they are also more likely to be aware of the effect of their environmental footprint than the average person.

As a lobbying group, birders have proven themselves a dedicated, hard-nosed lot. And they rank high among all conservation and outdoor groups in terms of their positive impact, not just for birds, but for the environment as a whole.

WHAT YOU CAN DO

The best way to make sure that you are the kind of birder that benefits rather than detracts from the environment is by developing an awareness of your own potential impact. Then, once you have considered all the ways in which you might have a negative effect you can set about reducing or offsetting it in some other way.

The bottom line is best expressed by the overarching aim of the American Birding Association's principles of birding ethics: 'In any conflict of interest between birds and birders, the welfare of the birds and their environment comes first.'

Should We Attract Birds with Recorded Song?

Recordings of bird song have come a long way in the past few years, and the quality of modern recordings is impressive indeed. Alongside that, new media such as coin-sized memory cards have made the recordings easily transportable; while the Internet has made them instantly sharable.

As with so much in our modern world of technology, the question now changes from whether we can use recorded song to attract birds to whether we should use recorded song to attract birds? There's no doubt that recorded song is an effective attraction for many bird species. The sounds of their own species will draw birds in, although away from their normal activities. We must question how much energy they will spend to make those diversions and how much additional threat from predators they might risk. Both questions are particularly pertinent during the mating season, when birds are already expending plenty of energy.

At the moment there's no evidence that we need a total ban on using recorded bird song, but there is a very strong argument for contemplating the potential impact prior to each use and monitoring such impacts carefully.

STRANGE PLACES FOR BIRDWATCHING

Everyone loves a list. Magazines thrive on them, shouting from their front covers about the hundred greatest this or that unveiled inside. Well, here's mine – a list of the strange places I've watched birds. Please accept one caveat before I begin: These are not necessarily my favourite spots for birding and they are certainly not the wildest, but they are, well ... a little odd.

To get started, there's a men's room in an office building in Harrisburg, Pennsylvania, along the Susquehanna River, with a window that offers no view from the outside but provides a grand scouting post out across the wide stretch of water. Waterfowl, wading birds and gulls seem never to cease flying by, almost as if on parade.

Meanwhile, across the state there's another office with lobby windows that offer the perfect vantage over a peregrine falcon nest on a ledge on an adjoining high-rise. My friend who works there is nearing retirement, so I had better think about cultivating a new contact who shares my passion.

Then there's the restaurant – which shall remain nameless – that serves the most atrocious food, but offers a view through an enormous glass window overlooking a pond that's reverted to wetland through sheer neglect. It's a haven for a constantly changing array of wetland birds. Luckily, the cook can produce a toasted cheese sandwich that is halfway edible and the soda pop from the fountain isn't chlorinated enough to be deadly.

HIGHWAYS AND BYWAYS

There's a spot along an interstate highway that I travel regularly where a bald eagle has somewhat incongruously taken up residence. I cruise by as slowly as the traffic, and the patience of the drivers behind me, permits.

There's a bridge with the narrowest of untended walkways on both sides of six lanes that tempts me into a reckless trek once or twice a year, when the herons and egrets nest by the dozens on an island just downriver. Not much further away, there's a huge electric transmission tower with a bald eagle nest about two-thirds of the way to the top. The birds are

The most unlikely places can hide unique birdwatching opportunities waiting for those who are willing to look beyond the obvious.

very tolerant of people as they approach via the dead-end roadway directly at the base of the tower.

There are fields in this one area of the Pennsylvania Dutch Country in Lancaster County, Pennsylvania, that year after year are particularly susceptible to flocking by thousands of blackbirds, starlings and grackles late in the summer. You can actually feel the beat of those thousands of wings when the flocks lift from the fields.

There are coal culm banks – mountains of waste dust piled in the wake of coal mining activity – that have eroded into sheer cliffs, into which colonies of swallows have tunnelled.

CLOSER TO HOME
Near where I live there are several home improvement stores with open-air, but under-roof storage areas that are particularly attractive to pigeons.

In my own back garden there's a butterfly house in my butterfly garden, which is spectacularly unattractive to butterflies but several years ago lured an industrious red-headed woodpecker to hack away at one of the slits it offers butterflies until it was enlarged into a rounded entrance hole. The woodpecker and its mate used the butterfly house just as they would a hollow tree. And other woodpecker pairs have followed their lead in subsequent years. It was an expensive addition to the garden that the butterflies never used – it's good to see someone getting benefit from it.

And lastly there's the interior of my house. We have a fairly wild landscape right up to the outside walls, including the front door, with plenty of scattered

Many common species of birds will make themselves right at home in our manmade environment, sometimes quite literally.

nestboxes. As a result there are often birds, such as chipping sparrows, mourning doves, robins and starlings nesting near the front door. And sometimes, when we're bringing in armfuls of groceries with the front door standing wide open, the birds find their way into our house. My wife makes certain that I watch them at that point.

I guess the point of all this is that the most unexpected places often provide the best opportunities. It doesn't matter if an exotic birding tour to far-flung parts is beyond your means, or that you regularly work a 12-hour day with a commute at either end. What really matters is that you keep your eyes open to the world around you, and the birds that share it with us.

THE FURTHER ART OF BEING HIDDEN

In addition to changing the comedy landscape the British television classic Monty Python's Flying Circus also gave some very sound instruction on one of birdwatching's prerequisite skills. A strange place perhaps to find such useful advice, but nevertheless the show's hilarious introduction to the art of remaining hidden holds a grain of truth.

The classic sketch in question was 'How Not to Be Seen'. Narrated by John Cleese, the supposed Government Training Film NO. 42 ran through various scenarios in which average people had attempted to hide under penalty of death if they were spotted. 'In this picture there are 47 people. None of them can be seen. In this film we hope to show you the value of not being seen,' began Cleese.

He then proceeded to trick several participants into showing themselves and paying the consequences in typically Pythonesque fashion. First among these is the unfortunate Mr. E. R. Bradford of Napier Court, Black Lion Road, London. The poor man is shot, with Cleese concluding that 'This demonstrates the value of not being seen.'

SOMETHING COMPLETELY DIFFERENT

Of course, the point to all this is that the Pythons, in the name of comedy, had hit upon some of the basics of watching birds successfully.

It's one thing to watch from afar with powerful binoculars, but if you want a closer, more intimate view then you have to understand how to hide yourself.

Aside from choosing appropriate cover, this entails drawing together a great number of the other skills that we've discussed elsewhere, not least among them patience and the art of staying still – both simple skills, but difficult ones to master. Thankfully, in the slightly gentler world of birdwatching the penalty for failure is a sense of frustration rather than instant death.

There are many different aspects to remaining hidden, choosing the right clothing being foremost among them.

📷 BIRDWATCHING IN THE RAIN

As the heavens open you can be sure that most birds, waterfowl apart, will hunker down under cover and stay as dry as they can. The challenge remains for you to keep dry without having to bolt for cover.

As birders follow the birds, we will all too often find ourselves amid the soaking, dripping vegetation in search of our quarry. It's against this constant rubbing and splashing that much waterproof clothing reveals its shortcomings – leaving you absolutely soaked to the skin.

I've had a little success against soaking legs with brush-gaiters – apparel which is generally more familiar to hunters than birders. I boost the waterproofing of my synthetic pair with multiple coats of silicone spray.

A similar treatment on synthetic rain jackets will enhance their water-shedding capacity. Often, however, the additional level of waterproofing will come at the expense of their capacity to wick sweat away from your skin. It's probably best to leave treating a new jacket or other item of waterproof clothing until its own waterproofing has started to fail, thereby extending its life.

Inclement weather conditions can lead to fascinating behaviour by birds, but at the same time can wreak havoc on delicate and expensive gear.

OPTICS

I wish there were as simple a solution for my glasses. Many birders will claim to prefer birding in the rain than in the wind, which can put the birds to roost to an even greater extent. However, eyeglass-wearing birders do not agree. Even with coatings of rain repellent and anti-fogging chemicals, we are often reduced to seeing little more than a hazy mist. As one participant in a particularly rain-soaked World Series of Birding once noted, imagine trying to birdwatch in a carwash. A baseball cap helps, unless the wind blows the rain in underneath.

Binoculars can simply be carried inside our jackets, but it's worth investing in a pair that incorporates a degree of waterproofing – something that's also worth considering when choosing a camera if you're going to be out and about in wet weather.

🔭 THE BIRDWATCHING TRIP

Grizzly bears, wolves, bison, elk, bighorn sheep and more were all part of our trip to Yellowstone National Park. But the tales that are told most often, a decade on, are about the grey jays that plagued us. Also known as 'camp robbers', the jays were our constant companions whenever a meal hit the picnic table. At first they were welcomed guests, entertaining us by accepting morsels right from our hands, but then they began to help themselves.

Apart from some local excursions to eagles' nests and ridgetop migration routes, I can't recall ever taking a major birding trip as such. I've taken plenty of nature trips and birds certainly have been significant parts of those, but only as part of the attraction. I can't really think of a single destination where I would travel and not take in all that nature has to offer, including the birds.

However, I can certainly appreciate the pull of a wildlife-watching vacation, a trip where the main aim is to enjoy wildlife in its natural environment. However, my wife doesn't see the appeal, holding that vacations are all about relaxation. We've come to terms with our difference of opinion and are lucky enough to take several different types of vacations each year.

BEFORE YOU GO

There was a time when taking a wildlife-watching vacation required incredible amounts of research, planning and flexibility – especially in a world without the internet.

That was all before the advent of what is now known as eco-tourism. The growing public interest in the environment, the pressure on governments around the world to make the most of their natural resources in a way that is sustainable, and the increasing ease of getting to

Eco-tours to places with exotic and unusual birds – such as these puffins to be found in the Scottish islands – have opened up a wealth of new opportunities to birders, while at the same time providing resources to conserve important habitats.

far-flung parts has all made a distant birding trip more easily attainable. The rapid growth in packaged eco-trips has also greatly reduced the planning that is required of you, sometimes to nothing more than reading a website and clicking the credit card button.

However, even with the trip already booked, pre-departure research is still the key to making the most of your time. Even in touristy spots such as Yellowstone it's entirely possible to miss worthwhile sites by relying solely on information provided by a tour company or on location. A bit of research online beforehand will almost always turn up some extra details, and this is even more the case with exotic birding destinations.

If you do want to focus solely on birds – although I can't see quite why you'd want to exclude the other things that your destination has to offer – the planning is even more critical. Make a list of all the species you want to see, and study their habits, habitats and behaviours in advance.

Once on site, don't focus so intensely on your planned objectives and itineraries that you miss the opportunities that present themselves unexpectedly. I've always been amazed at the events that unfold before my eyes when I just stop at some place new and watch and wait for a little while. It's a simple strategy that nearly always works, regardless of the location or the species you're searching for.

Taking a trip to somewhere new offers us sights we've never seen before. But just as interestingly, it also casts what we see closer to home in a new perspective. And a trip is worth it for that alone.

PERMISSION

The following is the simplest entry in this whole book. When it comes to birdwatching and private property, if you don't have permission to enter then don't. Nothing does more to bring about the complete closure of private property than unauthorised entry.

The saddest sight is a no-entry, private property sign on the edge of a property owned by someone who would never have posted the sign had the trespassers just asked permission. It's amazing just how much impact uninvited boots can have.

It's often the case that properties surrounded by such signs are actually still open to those who ask permission. I've gained access to countless such spots simply because I am willing to ask politely, even when the signs have appeared. The perceived impact of birders on a private owners' land is often much lower than other would-be users, so it's always worth enquiring.

📷 TRACKING

The history of tracking is ancient; in many ways it is as ancient as humanity itself as early hunters pursued their quarry across the grasslands, sometimes losing sight of it and being forced to turn to the signs of its passing for clues. Now tracking has developed an almost mystical aura, perhaps bolstered by the impressive sight of an expert drawing detailed conclusions from a bent branch, flattened grass or a muddy impression that the rest of us wouldn't give a second glance.

The stunning precision that you see from experts on television and in the field is what lies at the heart of great tracking, but it's not only an art for seasoned professionals – it's also a great pursuit for amateurs.

Snow is a great equalizer, and there's no better way for an amateur to get started than by examining a blanket of the white stuff. Few wild creatures can hide the evidence of their passing when snow covers the ground. The pheasant reveals the secret of its great escape ability. The owl leaves traces of its wings as it swoops on its hapless prey. Aside from birds, the daytime bed of the deer is there, a depression in the snow for all to discover. But even when there is no covering of snow, there is still plenty to be seen.

ON THE RIGHT TRACK

Observations similar to those made by professionals can help every one of us amateur naturalists to build our knowledge of wild creatures and wild places. A walk through the winter wood is an encyclopedia of wildlife details.

A good field guide to tracks and a journal to record observations are all the equipment that is needed.

Track study can be anything from a light afternoon's enjoyment, to a careful, painstaking affair aimed at extracting every bit of information from each impression in the snow or mud. But be warned: those who choose to follow the way of the tracker–naturalist are entering a world filled with both detailed information and infinite confusion, but one that also promises great reward.

Start slowly, really slowly. Walk slowly, stopping to examine every trace of a track. Worry not about wet knees; get down close to the track to drink in its every line, crevice and cranny.

Follow the trail for a little way, rather than making a quick identification and moving on to the next available imprint. The trail is where the habits, behaviours, haunts and burrows of what you are tracking will be revealed to you.

As Olaus J. Murie and Mark Elbroch explain in their more than useful book *Animal Tracks*, 'Reading tracks is not easy. Just as a detective, with certain broad principles in mind, finds each situation somewhat different, so the animal tracker must be prepared to use ingenuity to interpret what he or she sees. A track in the mud may look different from one in dust, or in snow, even if the same individual animal made them. A track in the snow is different after a warm sun has shone on it – enlarging and distorting it.'

It is these differences that make tracking so challenging a pastime, but in turn it is this challenge that provides such a great satisfaction when you finally realise you've got it right.

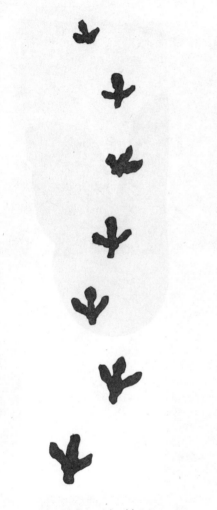

Birds that spend considerable amounts of time on the ground leave a great deal of evidence of their passing, as well as insights into their lives, in their tracks.

🔭 BIRDWATCHING ACCESSORIES

There are many passions that naturally require whole cases of accessories and gear. Fishing tackle boxes and camera bags seem to get larger every year, for example. Not so birdwatching.

Of course, there is plenty of kit that you can weigh yourself down with if you so wish. Many of these items are discussed elsewhere in this book, and there is certainly much usefulness that has come from the onward march of technology – birdsong players, cameras, and lightweight rain gear among them.

Yet, when you pause to think about it, what do we really need beyond a field guides, pair of binoculars and a notebook? And do we even need those? That's not to say that there isn't a place for birding technology, there certainly is, but sometimes it can distract from the point of our hobby. For a change, why not leave your kit at home? Why not just go out and watch birds?

FINDING GREAT PLACES TO WATCH BIRDS

Want to know where best to see birds? Look out the nearest window. Honestly, just about anywhere outside is a great place to watch birds. Some spots are better than others, some promise a great many more birds or a greater variety of species, while others will offer the chance to see a rare or unusual bird.

My current favourite spot for birdwatching is the road that leads into my development. An American kestrel that I once took to a wildlife rehabilitator after it was injured in a severe thunderstorm has returned and set up its territory there. Nearly every other day I pull over to the side of the road to watch him survey the damp grassland next to the road and sometimes dive for a helpless grasshopper. I'm there for the tiny hawk, but I'm lucky enough that every few days a great blue heron shows up to hunt through the small stream that meanders through the grassland, while red-winged blackbirds are almost always part of the scene.

A great blue heron often forms part of the scene at my favourite birding spot.

WHAT TO LOOK FOR

Exactly what makes a great place to watch birds depends on the species you're looking for. My own tastes lead me to small wetlands and ponds as far from roads as possible. Such locations generally offer a rich diversity of life in all its forms.

However, I never put any effort into finding the place from which I watch that kestrel. It was just a chance encounter with the stricken bird (see pp. 110–11) otherwise I'd probably just drive right on by to this day. That just goes to show the value of keeping your eyes open, as even the best-prepared birder can never rule out the influence of luck.

THE ART OF STAYING STILL

Patience is certainly a virtue that will serve any birdwatcher well, but when it's combined with an ability to remain absolutely still then it approaches a hallowed status – in the birding community at least. No matter how careful your camouflage, or how well placed your blind, you can be sure that an ill-judged movement will have your quarry taking to the skies like a shot.

Some naturalists have suggested that anyone unable to stay still for an hour should look outside of birdwatching for a new hobby. While such an ability is admirable and extremely useful, such a restriction is a little harsh for my tastes.

In this time of instant messaging, instant meals and instant entertainment, attention spans are waning and need to be rebuilt gradually – at least if you want to be a halfway decent birder. The reversion to such values of slowness will doubtless reap rewards for the patient birdwatcher, but these really need to be experienced rather than explained, if they are truly to capture a newcomer's interest.

STAYING STILL

The ability to remain still is hardly an innate ability. It must be acquired through practice, and a few simple methods are described on p. 10. Perhaps the most important thing is a sense of awareness, because much movement is the product of habits. Through a determined and conscious effort you can break these habits and become a better birder in the process.

How long can you be still? Test yourself some time. You may well be amazed at how little patience you have for this most important of birdwatching skills.

That said, comfort is also an extremely important factor to keep you from shifting needlessly. Dressing in appropriate clothes that will keep you dry, warm and comfortable helps no end. As does positioning yourself well to start with, so you don't find yourself fighting cramps as you struggle to keep your binoculars on the amazing specimen that's just fluttered into view. Furthermore, if you can carry a small pack-down stool with you, then that can make all the difference.

Finally, if you do have to move – that itch just has to be scratched, right? – then make it slow and steady.

🔭 BIRDWATCHING AT NIGHT

Lying in the muck and freezing, shallow water of the vernal pond, at the bottom of a bouncing, rolling tumble down a bank and over a log, with my flashlight beyond reach and doubtless sinking fast, I had begun to question the sanity of my little expedition.

Apart from a groan somewhere to my left, the friend I had talked into this nocturnal sojourn had no further thoughts to offer. The croak of the frog at the far end of the pond also did little to console my bruised and bloodied body or my equally battered ego. Then the great horned owl we had been closing in on let loose with another of its deep-throated booms and all was right with the world once again.

Birdwatching at night is like that. One wrong turn can lead to a world of pain and a questioning of one's own sanity. But the sound of just one bird can make it all worth your while.

NIGHT FLIGHT

The night is filled with the song and calls of myriad birds, such as the haunting voice of the nocturnal owls. This is particularly the case during the spring and autumn migration periods, when many songbirds make their flights at night to avoid the diurnal predators that abound. Although hazardous – as I found to my cost – wetlands and small ponds can be especially interesting, with the roosting waterfowl setting up a steady chorus.

Night migration takes place on such a scale that it is even a concern for wind farms, as bird collisions with the turbines seem to occur after dark. In fact several large studies have been conducted into the phenomenon, and you can read some of them online.

It's amazing just how much is on offer to the birder willing to stay up late, dozing on a camp stool with a mug of coffee, until an owl's haunting cry makes them sit bolt upright.

Birdwatching at night will unveil what appears to be a completely different world, along with an array of new and exciting sights and sounds.

🔭 SIZING UP A NEW SPOT

My home state of Pennsylvania offers a great many wonderful parks. The long carpets of manicured lawn between the statuesque rows of towering, mature trees are wonderful places to stroll, picnic and play. But after a few quick scans for anything unexpected, they are generally pretty dull places for birdwatching. They are monocultures to the extreme, offering an almost unparalleled uniformity of life, including birdlife.

Believe it or not, I find the roadsides leading to those parks are generally much more interesting. The patches of weeds in the ditches, the now feral former agricultural fields, the richly planted home gardens all are much richer in diversity, and therefore more interesting.

IN SEARCH OF DIVERSITY

The first step on coming to any new birding spot is a non-step. Stop and look around. Regardless of the location, every spot offers better and worse vantage points. Unless you're there in search of a particular bird, whose habits indicate differently, the place with the more diverse habitat will generally offer a much greater variety of birds to the first-time visitor.

With this in mind, the gradient where one type of habitat collides and mixes with another is almost always richer than either of the two habitats on their own. Also, water is a major attraction for birds, as are temporarily abundant sources of food, like a heavy crop of fruits or nuts.

AVOIDING PEOPLE

Aside from the fact that the presence of people will drive many birds away, heavy human use of an area will often leave it less diverse than before. Similarly, areas of human habitation generally only offer the same small variety of habitats, and therefore the same small variety of birds, as other urban areas.

The key lesson is to think like a bird. The factors you should look for in a habitat are the same as the bird will be looking for – a combination of elements that give a bird food, water, shelter and safety, all for the least effort.

Knowing what has made previous spots special in your birdwatching pursuits will help you to identify new places with plenty of promise.

BIRDWATCHING AND CAMPING

While a great many birdwatchers have simply lovely camping trips that take them into the wild and expose them to a smorgasbord of new bird species. I'm not one of them. While I've never been hired to set up my tent in a drought-stricken region, I do seem to have an unnatural ability to generate rain – long-lasting torrents of the stuff – wherever and whenever I pound in a tent stake. If you're looking for waterfowl, I might be a good camping buddy; otherwise, check my schedule and plan your outing for a different weekend.

On one of the rare occasions when I was camping 'sans la déluge', a pair of great horned owls serenaded the campgrounds each evening. It was a delightful taste of what non-rainmaking campers experience regularly.

During another of those all-too-rare instances when my pitched tent was actually dry for a few days in a row, a crow in the campground had developed a craving for bright, shiny objects. It sated that appetite with a regular stream of raids on the campsite when no one was about, making off with everything from bottle caps and nails to one unfortunate woman's sunglasses. Food left open atop picnic tables attracted all sorts of other moochers, but not that crow. He had his sights set firmly on greater treasures.

I can also remember a camping trip – with at least one dry morning – on which we woke to the sunrise chorus of at least a dozen woodland songbirds, maybe more. It was such an intense experience that we delayed the start of our day's activity – the very reason that we had risen so early in the first place.

I may not have the good fortune of spending many dry days, or for that matter nights, under canvas, but I have been camping for decades. Over that period I've developed a fairly thorough list of what I consider essential camping gear, so here it is.

+ A thick plastic sheet cut to fit the floor of the tent and placed on the ground under the tent enhances the comfort inside to an appreciable degree.
+ A thick air mattress placed atop a pad gives added insulation and provides an extra barrier against any moisture that does creep into the tent.
+ A tent repair kit and tent seam sealer.
+ A tarp or additional roofed enclosure for putting over the picnic table.
+ A spare tarp.
+ Replacement grommets.
+ Comfortable sleeping bags, liners and separate pillows.
+ Lawn chairs or camp chairs with good cushioning and of adequate size to offer true comfort!
+ A folding table, even if picnic tables are provided by the campsite.
+ Separate large plastic storage boxes, with secure lids, to store food and spare equipment.
+ Rope, string, twine and thread; all four to meet the various needs that will undoubtedly arise.
+ First-aid kit, with blister and sting/bite treatment, and a pair of tweezers.
+ A small shovel.
+ Paper towels, toilet paper, tissues, moist towelettes, aluminium foil and heavy-duty trash bags.
+ A hatchet.
+ A brush saw.

- A daypack.
- A can opener.
- A bottle opener.
- Food preparation gear, including sharp knives, a large spoon, a slotted spoon, a serving fork, a ladle, pots, pans, and coffee pot or tea kettle.
- A cuttingboard.
- A colander.
- A pot lifter and pot holders or insulated gloves.
- Plates, bowls, glasses, cups, knives, forks and spoons for eating.
- A tablecloth.
- A camp stove, at least a two-burner.
- Extra fuel for the stove.
- A lantern, preferably one that uses the same fuel as the camp stove.
- A grill for cooking over open fire.
- Long-handled fork and tongs for cooking over open fire.
- Dishpan, dishrack, dishwashing detergent, washcloths, towels and scrubbers.
- Food storage containers and resealable plastic bags.
- A flathead screwdriver, a cross-head screwdriver and a pair of pliers.
- A good length of wire.
- Duct tape.
- A sewing kit.
- Safety pins of various sizes.
- A small battery-operated or crank-powered radio.
- Extra batteries.
- Reading material, because it will rain.
- Playing cards and board games, because it will rain even more.
- A pad of paper or notebook, pens and pencils.

That might sound a lot, but I make no apologies. For me, comfort counts – even when camping.

Homemade Fire Lighters

Gather medium-sized pine cones that have already fallen from their trees. Keep them in some warm, dry, airy spot until they are brittle and bone dry. Wrap a bit of string around the pointed end of each cone. Melt wax and dip the cones into it. Let the wax begin to dry. Wrap some dryer lint around the cone and dip it again into the melted wax. Then place on waxed paper or aluminium foil and allow to dry. Store in a plastic bag.

Camping and birdwatching can be completely complimentary activities, each enhancing the experience of the other.

🔭 CARING FOR YOUR OPTICS

There's almost always a pair of binoculars somewhere in my vehicle. Maybe mixed in with the various maps, field guides and notebooks tossed on the back seat. Sometimes dangling from the rear-view mirror. Almost never in a pile of junk and candy wrappers on the floor of the car – really, that almost never happens. Now where did I leave them?

So, you get the picture of the kind of care I give, or rather don't give, to my optics. My real concern is to always have a pair of binoculars with me. Rather than investing in a fantastic pair which I then take special care of and worry about always having them close to hand, I prefer to have mid-level optics waiting for me just about everywhere I go – my vehicle, several windowsills around my house, my two offices outside the house, the potting shed, my camera bag and pretty much anywhere else I can find.

I recommend having a number of optics handy in various spots; but I wouldn't recommend the habitual lack of care I give them. It's ironic that many of us will trawl through catalogues and websites in search of the perfect pair, then spend a small fortune on them, only to treat them as if they are worthless. A much better plan is to give your optics great care right out of the box. The lens caps or rain guards (one-piece caps that cover both lenses) that come with the binoculars should be kept attached to it and over the lenses. Those caps or guards are the first line of defence against dirt, moisture and scratches. A case is supplied with the binoculars for the same reason. Although it's somewhat impractical in the field, the case should be used for general storage.

CLEANING OPTICS
Binoculars pick up specks of dust and bits of lint all the time, but not all of them need to be cleaned away immediately. Each cleaning you give a lens is another chance to scratch it, and not every speck is going to interfere with its optical performance. Clean the lens only when absolutely necessary. Blow off as much of the foreign material as possible with a blower brush and then brush it lightly with a lens brush. If this clears the dust, do nothing more. If it doesn't solve the problem, use a lens-cleaning cloth with a special lens-cleaning solution. Do not use eyeglass-cleaning solution; it can trash a lens.

Too much cleaning can be as bad as too little for quality optics, leading to just as many scratches. A simple blower brush should be enough to keep your lens free of most dust.

🔭 LIVING WITH SQUIRRELS

Most backyard birders seem to have a love–hate relationship with squirrels. It can range from blood-pressure-elevating rage when a squirrel enlarges the holes of a pricey feeder to get to the seeds within, to spirit-raising humour when that same bushy-tailed critter performs some acrobatic stunt.

Of course there are those who truly hate squirrels, but there are plenty more who could never envision a garden without them.

Every autumn I buy a hefty load of field corn, on the cob, from a local farmer to dump in towering mounds at various spots around my backyard just for them. This accomplishes two things: it maintains the squirrel population that I enjoy so much and it keeps them busy and away from my bird feeders, at least most of the time.

SQUIRREL-PROOF FEEDERS?

Not that I can't understand the frustration that many others feel. No squirrel-proof feeder has ever remained completely squirrel-proof forever, if it's hung where squirrels exist. Eventually, some squirrel will outwit the defences of the feeder, if only temporarily. Taking on the obstacles between themselves and their lunch is squirrels' stock in trade.

However, those backyard birders so inclined can spend a lot of money, time and energy to gain some temporary relief from the local squirrel population. Baffles around feeder poles will help a bit, as will moving the feeders beyond a squirrel's leaping distance from nearby trees. Feeders might be hung from a clothesline string with short sections of PVC pipe that will spin when a squirrel tries to move along the rope. Piano wire

Fame and wealth await the person who comes up with the bird-feeder device that really does thwart raiding squirrels.

or very heavy fishing line might be used to hang feeders. Limiting the amount of food put into the feeders at each refilling might allow the birds to eat almost all of the seed and leave little for the squirrels. Feeders equipped with spring-loaded, weight-triggered feeding holes will thwart squirrels for a while. Chew-resistant, metal cages around the feeding holes also will slow them down a bit.

The mixing of cayenne pepper with the bird seed has been recommended widely. It is said that the pepper doesn't bother birds, but sends the squirrels into fits – which seems a little mean to me.

Live-trapping the squirrels and releasing them 'somewhere else' is an option. However, where are you going to release them? Do you know someone who wants more squirrels on their property? Do wildlife regulations allow for the movement of squirrels by non-professionals? And, most pertinently, just how far must you move a squirrel to make sure it doesn't find its way back to your bird feeder?

🔭 MY FIRST AND FAVOURITE BIRDS

If I search my memory really hard – trawling through the dusty cabinets containing the memories of a great many days spent birdwatching – I come to a mockingbird in my parents' backyard at age six or seven. The backyard was small and narrow, and lined on both sides with thick hedges of thorny barberry. The mockingbird loved those hedges. Every year it attracted a mate, built a nest among the thorns and raised a new generation. And, even outside the mating and breeding season, the mockingbird fiercely defended that garden as its own against all comers: other mockingbirds, robins, other songbirds, cats and even dogs.

During those early years of my life, my mother was the birdwatcher in the family, thrilling at and sharing with me the joy of flocks of evening grosbeaks that turned up at our feeders in winter. The grosbeaks, which are birds of the north that irrupt south in lean times, seemed to make that southward flight more regularly back then. She was also especially keen on sighting little, bright yellow birds that she called 'salad birds', but that I now know as male American goldfinches.

Another bird I remember along the journey of my development as a birdwatcher was the indigo bunting. When the first one I ever saw paused on its northward migration one spring afternoon to take some seeds at a feeder on the balcony of my college dorm-room, I couldn't believe a wild bird could be so deep a blue. The image of that little bird is as vivid in my mind's eye today as it was first-hand a few decades ago.

A Close Encounter

Rather than a favourite species of bird, I actually have one particular bird that is my favourite. It's a male American kestrel that makes its home in the damp grasslands along the road leading to the development in which I live. Strange as it sounds, he's my favourite because we have a personal relationship.

A year ago, after a fierce storm had passed through the area, my son and I spotted the tiny bird lying on the ground, seemingly dead. As we regularly do with such sightings, we investigated more closely and discovered that the small hawk was in fact still alive.

However, we didn't want to touch the small predator without what we thought was proper safety gear. It was our first close-up, unsupervised encounter with any bird of prey. And although they were tiny, the bird's talons and beak looked more than capable of inflicting some nasty damage.

We hurried home and retrieved what we thought would serve as appropriate safety gear: a couple pairs of leather gloves, thick long-sleeved jackets, two pairs of safety glasses and a metal hamster cage with dry towels placed inside. Back to the bird we rushed, ready to fend off whatever attack it might mount when we tried to help it.

The kestrel made only slight movements with his head as my gloved hands closed around its surprisingly small and fragile body. With a laugh, I stripped off the gloves so I could handle the helpless little guy more carefully.

We wrapped the once-feared predator in the towel and raced to the nearest wildlife rehabilitator. A few anxious minutes later, his examination revealed that there was no lasting damage to the bird; it had perhaps suffered a concussion or something similar during the storm. A few weeks later, the rehabber called for us to pick up the bird and release it where we had found it. I used leather gloves to handle the bird and this time it snapped viciously at my fingers, as if to prove it was back to fighting strength.

I stop my vehicle along that road every few days and marvel at the kestrel, knowing I had a part, however small, in its still being there, occupying and defending that territory. I'm as proud as

Evening grosbeaks, on the occasional irruptions to the south, were special events to my kitchen-window birdwatching mother.

a father when I see that he's attracted a mate, and I'm as worried as a parent when I see a red-tailed hawk cruising his way.

It might seem a little soppy, but going through something like that with a bird, thinking that you're risking injury to help what would be a dangerous creature under other circumstances, you can't help but feel that a bond is formed. Sure, it may well be based on my misconceptions about the bird's sentience, but that doesn't stop it feeling special.

🔭 BIRDING VACATIONS

Nearly 10,000 species of bird are found across the Earth, which should be more than enough motivation for any serious birder to consider setting off for the four corners of the globe. Whether you're lucky enough to take an annual break, or you've saved hard for the trip of a lifetime, it's hard not to salivate at the thought of the big-name, must-see spots of birding travel.

South Africa with its thousand different species; the Pantanal and Amazon Rainforest of Brazil, with some of the rarest birds in the world; the wild northern coast of Costa Rica; the jungles of Belize; the tiny Caribbean island of Tobago, with more than 400 bird species; Antarctica and its tremendous populations of penguins. Whatever the destination, advance planning far beyond the brochures and itineraries provide by tour companies is the ticket to a successful and enjoyable vacation.

While every backyard has at least a few dozen bird species frequenting it, the Earth has more than 10,000 species and that requires some travel to say the least.

Thorough research often reveals potential additional trips that can be incorporated into your vacation by advance request.

GOING SOLO

Self-organised, self-guided birding vacations are not only possible, but for many preferable. So passionate have such vacationers become that entire books have been written to help in their planning and execution; you just have to hit the internet or get to your local bookstore.

However, while the printed page certainly has its uses, it's not a patch on the internet when it comes to up-to-date information. This is a wonderful resource for planning a birding vacation, but the ephemeral nature of the web means that it does pay to check your facts against another source – even just another website. That'll save you the unfortunate fate of falling prey to inaccurate information or even spoofs – after all, you wouldn't want to structure your holiday around a week's snipe hunting would you?

That said, official sites of birding charities or national organisations can generally be trusted to provide accurate information. And regional groups often have their own sites which are packed with useful information, and may also offer a great opportunity to meet up with some like-minded locals and even go birding with them.

Finally, it's worth buying any additional kit you need before you go, particularly when it comes to things such as field guides – you can't be sure you'll find them once you arrive.

👀 THE CALL OF THE WILD

Few things are more annoying in the outdoors than the piercing ring of someone else's phone. Few things are more comforting in the outdoors than the service bars of your own phone when you're late, lost or stranded. It's amazing just how different our perception of someone else's phone can be to that of our own.

Of course, simply selecting the mute button or keeping your phone switched off until you need it is the most straightforward solution – and will avoid the embarrassment of your tacky ringtone causing entire flocks to take to the air.

However, phones are being put to ever-more inventive uses, not least within the birding world. Paid alert services can zip details of the latest sightings to your handset, and in some instances hundreds, even thousands, of birders have shown up on the spot within just a few hours of an alert being sent.

Indeed, so pervasive have phones become that the annual World Series of Birding in New Jersey now bans their use for anything other than obtaining weather and traffic information. Contact with local birding hotlines is strictly forbidden.

RECORDING BIRDSONG

For a pastime with what is mostly a genteel image, birdwatching boasts plenty of controversial areas for passionate debate. Whether or not you should use recorded calls as lures is just one such hot topic, but the recording of calls themselves stretches back to the late nineteenth century.

Ludwig Koch is often credited as the first person to record birdsong, something he is said to have done at the age of just eight in 1889. His subject was the Indian shama, a member of the thrush family, and his later work with E.M. Nicholson, director of the Nature Conservancy, led to a book, *Songs of Wild Birds*, and a base of recordings that subsequently launched the BBC's natural history library.

From those beginnings a miniature industry developed and the late 1920s saw the beginnings of sound recording at the Cornell Lab of Ornithology. Although such early technology was limited, and the quality of the recordings was relatively low, it did generate great interest. Indeed, many technological innovations later, the Macaulay Library at Cornell (until 2000 the Library of Natural Sounds) now stands as the world's largest collection of recorded birdsong, boasting 170,000 recordings of 75 percent of the world's bird species.

More than a hundred years on, relatively cheap and compact equipment has made this intriguing aspect of birding more easily accessible. Give it a go yourself, there is so much more to hear than you can possibly imagine.

In truth, it's not quite this easy, but there are some fascinating techniques for recording birds' many calls and songs.

Song versus Call

Songs generally are more musical and complex, produced by the male as part of the mating ritual. Calls are generally less musical and somewhat simpler. They are used to communicate much among and between the birds, including territorial warning, the urge to flock, aggression, the location of food and more. Calls relate more to the present situation of the bird than do songs.

🔭 GONE PISHING

Pishing is the imitation of a generic bird call to attract birds. It sounds something like 'pish-pish-pish'. It's a standard tool in the repertoire of many a birdwatcher and researcher alike, as it is attractive to a wide array of bird species.

The reasons for its effectiveness are widely debated. Many believe it mimics the danger or mobbing call of common species such as tits – a call to which a wide variety of prey species will respond. Acoustical analysis has shown it to fall into the frequency range of those natural sounds. And, pishing is often ineffective in parts of the world not inhabited by tits and chickadees.

Another theory for the effectiveness of pishing holds that it mimics the sounds made by birds inviting others to join in a mixed foraging flock, where the overall safety will be enhanced by greater numbers of eyes watching for predators.

To Pish or Not to Pish

So those are a couple of thoughts about why pishing works, but whether or not we should use it is another matter. Like the use of recorded song to attract birds, there are those who frown on even the simple act of pishing. They charge that it interferes with and disrupts the natural rhythm and behaviour of the birds. On the whole, however, it is less contentious – but it still pays to think first and pish second.

A simple 'pish-pish-pish' through human lips will cause a wide variety of bird species to reveal themselves to you.

THE PHYSICS OF FLIGHT

Birds were not the first creatures to take to the air. Insects have been flying for much longer, while there were winged dinosaurs and pterosaurs around at the same time as the first birds. However, birds have developed their flying abilities beyond any other group of living things. And it's also worth noting that they're better flyers than any machine built by humans.

Flying creatures have changed over the ages, but the laws of physics have not. Just like the first flyers, the birds of today need to balance the various forces in order to get into the air and fly.

THE FORCES AT PLAY

In order to get off the ground a bird must generate sufficient thrust from its wings to overcome its own weight. Then, once it is airborne, the flow of air over the wings provides lift. Working in opposition to this is drag, which is simply the technical term given to wind resistance.

Anyone looking closely at a bird's wing will notice that it is far from flat. It's actually nature's aerofoil, and boasts a greater surface area on its top than its bottom. This means that air passing over the top of the wing moves faster than that which passes underneath creating a pressure difference that gives the effect of lift.

ON THE WING

Another force that birds would need to concern themselves with, if they thought about such things at all, is known as 'wing loading'. It refers to the relationship between body mass and wing area, and it helps to explain why birds like swallows and swifts are able to stay airborne for much longer than heavy-bodied birds such as pheasants.

These competing demands account for the huge variety of wing shapes on show in the natural world: pheasants have short wings suited for explosive launches but slow flight; waders wings are pointed with sharper backward angles, which are no good for fast takeoffs, but great when it comes to gliding in

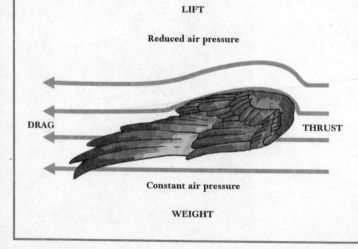

LIFT

Reduced air pressure

DRAG

THRUST

Constant air pressure

WEIGHT

The shape of a bird's wing is designed to maximise lift and thrust, while minimising weight and drag. To this basic template each species adds its own variations.

for a gentle landing; the big gliders, such as eagles and vultures, have long and broad wings, ending in feathers that separate like fingers and lend incredible control; while albatrosses have long, thin wings perfect for gliding low over the sea for great distances, taking advantage of even the slightest change in wind.

The shapes of individual feathers are also critical. Contour feathers, the outermost feathers that give a bird much of its colour and shape, are generally rigid and strong, providing the bird with support in flight. Each contour feather is connected to the bird by a set of muscles, which controls its position.

The largest contour feathers, which also happen to be the dominant flight feathers, are called the 'remiges'. The primary remiges – the largest, strongest and outermost – often have the appearance of fingers when spread, while the inner (secondary) remiges do the yeoman's work in soaring and flapping. Meanwhile, at the back end, tail feathers, known as the 'rectrices', provide stability and control.

With all that physics at play it's a wonder that birds get off the ground at all. But when they do we are left with little choice but to marvel at the breathtaking skill on display.

Make a Contribution

How much did you contribute to conservation and research over the past year? And I don't mean through taxes or fees. With most bird organisations, I guess registration fees may be counted, as these institutions usually make good use of every penny they can get; but beyond that how much did you give?

While those with conflicting interests continue to debate the implications of global climate change and the actions, or reactions, it requires, those of us in the field know that something big is happening. To anyone setting foot in the wild, it's obvious that major change is taking place, and it doesn't look good.

We've reached the point where we have run out of alternatives. The time for never-ending debate has passed as we're losing species and coming close to losing entire ecosystems. The sad fact of the matter is that we're going to lose more, and there's nothing we can do to change that.

On a brighter note, there is much that can still be saved. There are even some ecosystems that can be recovered, returned to their former state, or at least something approaching it. However, action in our modern world requires money, and if we want future generations to be able to enjoy our hobby then it's up to us to put our hands in our pockets before time runs out.

🔭 BIRDWATCHING AT CHRISTMAS

Although much of our attention is drawn to family, friends and festivities around Christmas time, the holidays present some great opportunities for sharing with our extended feathered family.

For example, I for one, have always felt that the Christmas fruit cake does not deserve its bad reputation. However, I do seem to be the only person who truly enjoys it, so I can only assume there are many homes with a sad looking cake sitting uneaten after the holidays.

Thankfully, many garden birds vindicate my opinion of all those great bits of fruits and nuts surrounded by tasty cake. Just chop the fruit cake into tiny pieces, scatter them on a sheet of waxed paper or aluminium foil and allow them to stand exposed to the air for a day or two. When they have reached a dry, crumbly stage, scatter them on the ground at the base of your feeders.

With the holiday break drawing to a close, the fruit bowl probably holds some sorry-looking offerings; while the pantry doubtless contains the odd half-bag of stale snacks; and the tin of Christmas cookies is now all crumbs and fading freshness. All those holiday leftovers can be cut up and scattered for use by the eager critters. Moreover, things like popcorn, cereal and dried fruit can be strung together to make edible garlands that can be hung around your garden.

RECYCLE YOUR TREE

On the last day of the break, when the decorations are coming down, do something environmentally sound with your old Christmas tree.

Drag it out into the backyard and prop it trunk-up at a 30- to 60-degree angle against a bird-feeder pole or a similar support. Wire it loosely in place to prevent strong winds from carrying it into a neighbour's yard.

For the rest of the winter the tree will provide shelter to a wide variety of songbirds and small critters. Then when spring comes, chop up the twigs, branches and trunk for mulch.

Share your holiday treats with the birds and they will fill your garden with their own colourful, decorative presence.

🔭 BIRDWATCHING IN THE HEAT

Look closely when you're watching birds during the hottest days of summer and you will see some amazing mechanisms being employed as they work to regulate their body temperatures. Bathing in whatever water might be found is only the most obvious method of cooling.

Birds lack sweat glands and so employ a great variety of techniques to avoid overheating. Aside from the obvious bathing, and the slightly less obvious, but nonetheless ubiquitous panting, this can be one of the most fascinating areas of bird behaviour.

Among the many schemes employed is the way in which nesting gulls keep themselves facing the sun throughout the day, reducing the area of their bodies exposed to the sun's rays. Meanwhile, very few of us will be granted the dubious honour of seeing a vulture excreting onto its own legs, so that it will cool it as it evaporates. These are just two of a vast array of fascinating behaviours you can see, you just have to remember to keep cool yourself.

Hot Spots

It's amazing that in spite of the rocketing temperatures birds are able to survive in an incredible diversity in some of the hottest places on Earth. For example, Death Valley National Park – which in Death Valley itself has recorded temperatures as high as 134 °F (56.7 °C) – boasts nearly 400 species of bird, while the Western Sahara boasts around 200 different species.

Few places on Earth – including the hottest, driest deserts – are devoid of at least a few species such as the resilient roadrunner found in the Americas.

BEST BIRDWATCHING SPOTS

What makes one spot great but excludes another? You only have to flick through a wildlife magazine, search the web or chat to a friend to find a passionate debate about where the best place to go to see a particular bird is, but are things really that simple?

Fame or fortune are the motives for many of the websites that promise readers their take on where's best. While for an individual there is often a touch of sentimentality.

THE PERSONAL TOUCH

Certainly, the initial response for many of us is to reel off a list of the big name, exotic locations we've managed to visit or heard about from a fellow birder. However, if we pause for a moment, our minds may drift to the local, familiar, lesser-known spots. In other words, for many of us, our favourite and regular haunts are our best birdwatching spots.

I'm rather proud of the habitat that I've recreated in my backyard, which is certainly one of my best birdwatching spots. On a similarly personal note, I live within a 30-minute drive of the world-famous Hawk Mountain Sanctuary – the world's first sanctuary exclusively for birds of prey – and I've volunteered and presented programmes there, so it's another favourite. My family vacations each summer in southern New Jersey, have made me familiar with another world-famous spot, Cape May, and if I think about it there's a personal link of one kind or another to all of the other locations that would grace my list.

Of course, the web is unparalleled in offering lists, information and advice on where to go to be sure of seeing a particular bird. But is that what really makes any one spot great? Surely, it's that personal connection, the joy that you can feel at watching birds in an environment where you feel at home.

Lists of the best birding spots can be found quite easily on the newsstand or the internet. But even the best researched list will lack the personal connection that can make a site feel truly special to each of us.

THE MOST ELUSIVE BIRDS

As I write, the ivory-billed woodpecker of the American southeast may be the most elusive bird on the planet. There have been a handful of heavily disputed sightings and audio-recordings and that's it for the whole of the twentieth century. A sizable community discounts the reputed spottings as being mistaken and still believe the ivory-bill to have gone extinct before the turn of the previous century, which would certainly make the job of those wanting to spot it a little bit harder.

There's good reason for wanting to prove the continued existence of a bird that has been described by some as the 'Lord God Bird' because that was often the exclamation of those seeing a wild specimen for the first time.

HIDE AND SEEK

Remoteness of habitat is one reason for a bird's elusiveness. The ivory-billed woodpecker, if it does indeed still exist, inhabits large tracts of swamp, which make tracking the bird on the ground nigh-on impossible. A less-palateable reason – at least to those of us who care about the environment – is the increasing rarity of many species. Sadly, global climate change, not to mention deforestation and the encroachment of humankind on those dwindling areas that are truly natural, will see more and more species of bird becoming more and more elusive.

Debate continues to rage over whether the ivory-billed woodpecker, thought to be extinct, may have been sighted in the southeastern U.S.

Then when things are pushed beyond breaking point, the euphemism of 'elusive' as a less distasteful synonym for endangered becomes redundant. A bird simply becomes extinct and vanishes, never to be seen again.

At least that is the case more often than not. However, it is not unknown for the occasional species to be reprieved in a manor similar to the much-hoped-for rediscovery of the ivory-billed woodpecker. One such example being the recently re-discovered Beck's petrel of Papua New Guinea.

Of course, on more than one occasion I've attributed much more common and close-at-hand birds with the trait of elusiveness, particularly when everyone but me on a birding excursion was able to spot them.

BEYOND THE LIMITS

If you spend any time reading other birders' life-lists, online discussion groups of bird sightings and the like, you're certain to run into the word 'extralimital'. Without these birds that somehow find their way beyond their normal limits, life-lists would be generally much shorter, and birdwatching less thrilling.

The term extralimital can relate simply to a bird that is found outside its normal geographic range. However, it can also be used in a seasonal sense, when the species may be found there at other times of the year, but not usually when the sighting has been made.

Major storms are a common cause of extralimital sightings, and online groups will often experience a boom in activity in the wake of a storm that has pushed birds beyond their normal territories. Likewise, sudden changes in habitat whether caused by humans or nature (as can often be the case with large forest fires) can push birds in new directions.

THE CASE OF THE RUFOUS HUMMINGBIRD

Extralimital sightings can also be the indication of something new happening within a species. And this may well be the case with rufous hummingbirds in the U.S., and the Hummer/Bird Study Group is watching closely.

The group has bird banders working in various parts of the country, catching and banding rufous hummingbirds. This is generally a western species but it has been showing up nearly as far as the opposite coast with increasing regularity. It appears the birds are developing a new wintering ground in southern Georgia, the Florida panhandle and west into Texas – a big variation from their normal wintering grounds in Mexico.

This behaviour was first noticed in the mid-1970s and attributed to boomerang migration, in which the birds were making the trip to their normal spots in Mexico but then veering back north into the southern U.S. However, the group's work is showing that the birds are actually following a new migration route east from the Pacific northwest into the mid-Atlantic states and then south into the Gulf region. At the same time, there also appears to be a genetic mutation taking place that inclines the little birds towards their new wintering grounds.

Extralimital hummingbirds almost always cause a big stir in local birdwatching communities, but some out-of-range birds may be in the process of expanding the range.

With the climate growing warmer and more gardens being created in the southeast, birds with that genetic modification are surviving where they may not have been able to survive a few years ago, and in doing so creating more of their species with the same genetic inclination. If the trend continues, then some day in the future the species may no longer be considered extralimital in those parts.

OTHER CAUSES

Let's face it: just as in humans, not every bird is equally equipped in the brains department. Most such birds do not survive long enough to make an extralimital mark; however, some do luck their way past enough predators and other hazards to travel far enough in the 'wrong' direction to make it onto someone's life-list.

Only time ever reveals whether an extralimital bird is the brave pioneer forging new territory, or simply lost.

A further consideration with any extralimital is the possibility of its escape or release from captivity. Unfortunately, there are always going to be those bird fanciers that move birds in their cages over very long distances. Breakouts are not infrequent, birds do escape regularly; but like those that find themselves in unfamiliar surrounds through inauspicious winds or navigational error they are often not long for this world.

Should I Tell Others?

We've touched upon it earlier, but it's an issue that's worth coming back to. Time and again, someone locates an extremely rare bird, a bird that many, many others want to see personally. Word spreads quickly – in these modern times, often as fast as a broadband internet connection – and, suddenly we have the birdwatching equivalent of a celebrity red carpet.

Crowds, parking problems and the like all mark the area within which the bird can be found. Unlike celebrity hotspots, however, the owners of such a birdwatching hotspots may not be all that happy about the situation.

The question of spreading the word about a bird sighting is a critical one. It's nice to share with others of course, and it's undeniable that there's a certain prestige to being the first to report a rare bird. Face it, you've more than likely benefitted from similar reporting by others.

However, there is a downside to all of this, and the impact of your report must be considered. Will the pressure of additional birdwatchers be detrimental to the habitat or the landowner's property? And, most importantly, will the impact have some negative effect on the bird at the centre of the excitement? All of these are questions that you must weigh very carefully in your mind, because once you let the cat out of the bag, there's no getting it back in.

🔭 BIRDWATCHING MYTHS

Myths and legends are a part of any hobby; they find form in the cliché of the angler's 'one that got away', tales that are listened to, repeated, embellished and exaggerated. I have no doubt that the internet has brought about a vast increase in myths and myth-spreading. It's even given birth to websites that are dedicated solely to debunking and tracking myths, many of which seem destined to live on regardless.

You all know you should discontinue your backyard feeding efforts in late summer through early autumn to avoid causing birds to forego their normal migrations, right? The basic assumption being that the foods we offer are so much better than what is out there naturally. But is it really possible that birds have become so dependent on our generosity that they simply will choose not to follow the cycles of a thousand generations.

FOOD FOR THOUGHT
Food-related myths are among the most popular. First among them is that birds become dependent on your backyard feeders and will starve if you stop your feeding effort in winter. Again, how dependent do you think those birds really are on your handouts?

Then there's the old, if slightly gruesome, tale that rice thrown at weddings will be eaten by birds and will then swell up in their stomachs until their guts explode and kill them. What do the tellers of this tale suppose is the difference between the kernels thrown at the end of a nuptials ceremony and the rice growing in the fields and being stolen en masse by wild birds?

In a similar, although presumably fizzier vein, comes the myth that effervescent antacid tablets fed to a gull will explode inside the birds, possibly to the extent that the explosion will be visible from the

ground. And inevitably to back the tale up comes the second-hand testimony of a friend of a friend of a brother-in-law once removed. Could you really take it that seriously? Have you ever seen the junk gulls eat? A little antacid may be just what the doctor ordered.

On a slightly more scientific note is the claim that purple martins eat a couple of thousand mosquitoes per bird per day. Actually, there's a grain of truth in this one, but it's based on studies of the stomach contents of a limited number of martins that were extrapolated. It sort of overlooks many other studies that have found mosquitoes, which are largely nocturnal, to be only one small part of the diet of the martin, which is in any case a day flyer.

AND ANOTHER THING
Bird myths aren't limited to their diets. There are the classic myths of yore including the phoenix that arises reborn from the flames, the Asian roc that dines upon elephants, and the halcyon that lends its name to days that are so calm it can make a nest on the still waters of the ocean.

However, such romantic notions are no longer believed. Instead, slightly more prosaic, but equally laughable, ideas persist about ruby-throated hummingbirds being too small to migrate on their own, hitching rides on the back of Canada geese. Exactly what's in it for the geese? And just how do the hummers hold on?

Back down to Earth, and birds' love lives provide fertile ground for speculation. But the stereotype of the swan pining after the death of a mate is largely unfounded. Indeed, swans sometimes have more than one partner, and they're not even particularly picky about them – with a rare black swan named Petra once taking up with a pedal boat in a German zoo.

Perhaps the closest to the classic legends of great birds that we have today is that of the giant eagle. The exact species changes from one tall story to the next, but invariably this king of the skies swoops and carries off some suitably impressive prize, be it a large dog, a deer or even a child. All with an effortless flap of the wings.

Doubtless these myths will continue, and I suppose for the most part they're pretty harmless. But if you do ever find yourself getting suckered in by one, don't say that I didn't tell you first.

The bald eagle is nowhere near as noble, majestic or brave as it was assumed to be when anointed the national symbol for the U.S.

INDEX

*TO MY MOTHER, WHO
LAUNCHED MY ENTHUSIASM;
TO MY SON, CASEY, WHO
NOW SHARES THE PASSION*